The Designing for Growth Field Book

The Designing for Growth Field Book:
a step-by-step project guide

Jeanne Liedtka, Tim Ogilvie, and Rachel Brozenske

Columbia Business School
Publishing

Columbia University Press
Publishers Since 1893
New York   Chichester, West Sussex
cup.columbia.edu
Copyright © 2014 Jeanne Liedtka, Tim Ogilvie, and Rachel Brozenske
All rights reserved

Library of Congress Cataloging-in-Publication Data

Liedtka, Jeanne.
    The designing for growth field book: a step-by-step project guide / Jeanne Liedtka, Tim
Ogilvie, and Rachel Brozenske.
        pages cm
    ISBN 978-0-231-16467-2 (pbk. : alk. paper) — ISBN 978-0-231-53708-7 (e-book)
1. Creative ability in business. 2. Organizational change. 3. Success in business. I. Ogilvie, Tim. II.
Brozenske, Rachel. III. Title.
    HD53.L544 2014
    658.4'063—dc23

                                                                                2013027797

Columbia University Press books are printed on permanent and durable acid-free paper.
This book is printed on paper with recycled content.
Printed in the United States of America

    c   10   9   8   7   6   5   4   3   2   1

References to websites (URLs) were accurate at the time of writing. Neither the author nor
Columbia University Press is responsible for URLs that may have expired or changed since the
manuscript was prepared.

Using Your Field Book

Welcome!

Chances are, if you bought this book, you are facing a messy challenge—and want to use design thinking to create an innovative solution. We have written this field guide to make that process easier, to create a road map for you to manage your innovation project as it unfolds.

A few years ago, Jeanne and Tim wrote *Designing for Growth: A Design Thinking Tool Kit for Managers* (D4G) with the goal of making design thinking tools and methods accessible to any manager interested in using them. Since then, we've learned some new things. Having spent that time helping hundreds of managers tap into design's potential, we saw an opportunity to get even more practical by creating a step-by-step guide. This is that guide—your field book. If you'd like more detail on the design thinking philosophy, you'll find that in D4G. If you own it already, you'll see that it serves as a great companion to this field book. But we think you'll find this field book is a useful guide to managing your project regardless of whether you have read D4G.

In D4G, we laid out a simple process that asked four questions:

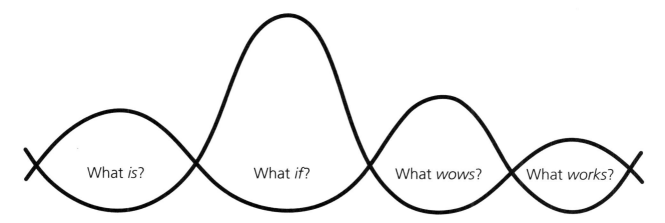

What *is*?   What *if*?   What *wows*?   What *works*?

What *is* explores current reality. **What** *if* envisions a new future. **What** *wows* makes some choices. **What** *works* brings us to action. We have built this step-by-step guide around those same four questions, with some reminders about the tools and project management aids we talked about in D4G, and the addition of a few new tools and aids.

We designed this field book for active use. You might ask, "What does that mean?" It means that it's not meant to stay pristine and pretty. Instead, write in it. Turn down the corners of the pages you like. Tear out the pages you can't stand. Doodle. Make notes in the margins. Stack and store your sticky notes. But most of all, keep it handy for whatever thoughts occur to you along the way.

Let's get started.

Although you can use your field book however you like, we suggest that it's particularly useful for three things.

Choosing

A successful design thinking experience begins with a great problem. Before you begin working the four questions, take time to choose a meaty challenge and frame your challenge question. The design brief form and instructions in Steps 1 through 3 of this field book will help you get set up for greatness.

Planning

Every challenge is different, so even with a handy guide like this you'll want to take time to plot your course. Being a good catalyst for problem solving requires planning. Think about which tools will be best suited to your challenge and the people who might be available to help you.

Good news: The steps and tools in this book will guide you along the way. We've also included an example project with completed templates in the final section if you find yourself lost in translation.

Doing

Thinking is fine, but it's also important to deliver results. At some point, you'll need to bring a team together and use the tools you've chosen to navigate your challenge. Grab a flip chart and some markers, follow your plan, use the tools, adjust it if you hit a bump in the road, and see where the journey takes you. This field book is your guide as you take on today's challenge, but you have a lifetime ahead of you to think like a designer.

Along the way, you can also visit Design@Darden, an online portal with more tools (including digital templates and ready-to-print posters) to help you get the action started.

Table of Contents

What you'll find in this field book. And where.

The Four Questions

What *is*?

Because our goal in addressing a challenge is to envision and implement an improved future state, it is always tempting to jump right to the future and get started solving. Many managers have been taught that creative thinking starts with brainstorming solutions. But the design process is human-centered and starts with the present, not the future—it begins with what is happening now. Innovative ideas are generated from insights about the current reality for real users, and without those insights, the imagination starves. That is why the **What *is*** stage is so important.

What *is* starts with the identification of the right kind of problem for design thinking to solve. Then it creates a design brief to move us into action. This stage ends with the identification of design criteria that point the way toward opportunities that were always there but were hidden. We call this the reframe. The reframe feeds the imagination for the next stage: **What *if.*** By taking the time to develop deep insight into your problem or opportunity and its context before you start trying to generate solutions, you are also establishing the reference point for change, the constraints that shape it, and the criteria for what success looks like.

What *if*?

Once you have thoroughly explored and documented **What *is***, you can look toward the future and one of our favorite questions: **What *if*?** The **What *if*** stage looks like the kind of creative and generative process that we expected design thinking to be all along, but it's surprisingly disciplined in its approach. This is because we want to push beyond simplistic expressions of new possibilities (the kind of output that an initial brainstorming session might produce) and arrive at robust concepts that can be evaluated, prototyped, and (if promising enough) developed.

Initially, the idea of activities like brainstorming makes most managers nervous. It is not the kind of thinking that we are trained in either at school or at work. Instead, we are trained to think critically, to debate and poke holes. This kind of critical thinking is important—but not yet!

A lot of research tells us that if we allow that kind of judging into our process too early it will drive creative ideas right out the door. An important part of asking **What *if*?** involves putting those hole-poking skills on hold and exploring a wide range of possibilities. Successful design thinkers use clever mental tools and tricks to get out of the habit of breaking things down and criticizing them.

What *is*?   What *if*?

What *wows*?

By the time we ask **What *wows*,** we have covered a lot of territory. Through the exploration of **What *is*,** we learned about the stakeholders we hope to serve. Through brainstorming and concept development in **What *if*,** we have homed in on some concepts that we believe have real potential to create value for our stakeholders and meet organizational objectives at the same time. Now it is time to make hard choices, identifying the best concepts—those that wow—in order to guide our next steps.

Typically, the "wow zone" for a business concept occurs at the intersection of three criteria: your targeted stakeholders want it, you are able to produce and deliver it, and doing allows your organization to achieve its objectives.

To assess whether your new ideas have the potential to wow, you start by identifying the key assumptions that must hold true for your concepts to be successful and the data you'd need to test them. You'll look at the data you've already got to work with. Then, you create a prototype of your ideas that will allow you to engage your stakeholders and get some high-quality feedback. This will set the stage for our final question, **What *works*?**, when you take these concepts into the field and actually test your assumptions with stakeholders.

What *works*?

This is the final stage of the design process—when your exciting high-potential concepts come face-to-face with your actual stakeholders in the real world. It represents the key difference between invention and innovation: Invention is doing something in a novel way; innovation requires that the invention be implemented and create value. Invention doesn't necessarily produce better outcomes for real people; only innovation does that.

We are all tempted to fall in love with the new concepts we have nurtured so carefully in the first three stages of the process. And we have stressed the idea of keeping many options open—but in real life we know it is too expensive to keep all our options open and try everything. Yet when you develop just one concept, you are apt to come up empty-handed if your key stakeholders are not interested in your masterpiece. The choice of which concepts to move forward is best *not* left to the same person who created them (you!). The right person is the same one who inspired you in the first place: the customer.

Instead of observing targeted stakeholders as they navigate the world of **What *is*,** you now need them to take a walk with you into several possible futures—and to engage them in co-creating a solution with you. This means putting your prototypes in their hands and refining them on the basis of their input until you arrive at a version that is ready for proof-of-concept testing in the marketplace, using the learning launch tool. This final step of the journey will give you enough information to make more solid data-based investment decisions.

What *wows*?   What *works*?

The Steps

Step 1: Identify an Opportunity

So that's it! Four simple questions. And we're ready to get started. We'll begin by making sure you've got the right kind of problem to work on.

As you identify your growth opportunity, it's important to consider whether design thinking is a fit for solving it. Design thinking is an approach to solving problems especially suited to conditions of high uncertainty. It is a set of methods that manage risk by placing small bets fast. This approach is not suitable for every challenge. In many cases, more linear methods may work better. For operational challenges where the required change is more incremental and where we have good data from the past that allows us to predict the future, we often find traditional analytic methods to be more resource efficient. The table shown at right will help you choose an opportunity that is suited to the unique methods of design thinking.

Think about Zipcar, the innovative car-sharing service. The original creation of Zipcar was an ideal fit for design thinking. The firm set out to create a new category of transportation service: car rental by the hour, with an element of social responsibility through resource sharing. More than a year after Zipcar proved its model in the dense urban context, it sought to extend its service into small university towns. This follow-on challenge could be addressed with more linear analytic methods, since the year-plus of operating data from urban markets could help eliminate many of the unknowns.

So, as you choose where to play, use the six questions as a guide to find your opportunity.

Write down an area of opportunity you think you might like to explore:

Now ask yourself the following questions:

Question	Design thinking is appropriate if …	Linear analytic methods may be better if …
Is the problem human-centered?	Deep understanding of the actual people (users) involved is both possible and important	There are few human beings involved in the problem or the solution
How clearly do you understand the problem itself?	We have a hunch about the problem and/or opportunity, but we need to explore and get agreement	We understand the problem clearly and are sure we're solving the right one
What's the level of uncertainty?	There are many unknowns (large and small), and past data is unlikely to help us	The past is a good predictor of the future
What's the degree of complexity?	There are many connecting and interdependent facets of the problem; it's hard to know where to start	The path to solving the problem is clear, and analytic methods have succeeded in solving similar problems in the past
What data is already available to you?	There is very little relevant existing data to analyze	There are several clear sources of analogous data
What's your level of curiosity and influence?	I'm excited to explore more and can get a group of people willing to help me	The problem feels routine to me, and I have to follow existing processes and systems

Step 2: Scope Your Project

Framing a project and refining its scope are crucial for effectively pursuing new opportunities. Use the framework on the facing page to expand (or focus) your thinking about your project.

Start by thinking about your project in terms of the area of opportunity you want to explore, and write that in the center box. Try to start your statement with an action verb. (For example, if you're working to improve online ordering for a clothing retailer, your initial statement could be something like, "Help people buy clothes for work.")

Then, explore your project from both broader and narrower perspectives. Is there a higher-level challenge out there that might unlock more opportunity? ("Help people look and feel great.") Is there a more focused project that would address a specific barrier that needs to be addressed? ("Help people ensure that online purchases fit.")

Even when your project definition seems really clear, it's worth exploring the reasons and barriers to make sure you're aiming at the right opportunity. Once you've looked both broad and narrow, select a project scope that feels actionable, with enough possibility to make it interesting and enough traction that you can do something about it.

Jot your notes here:

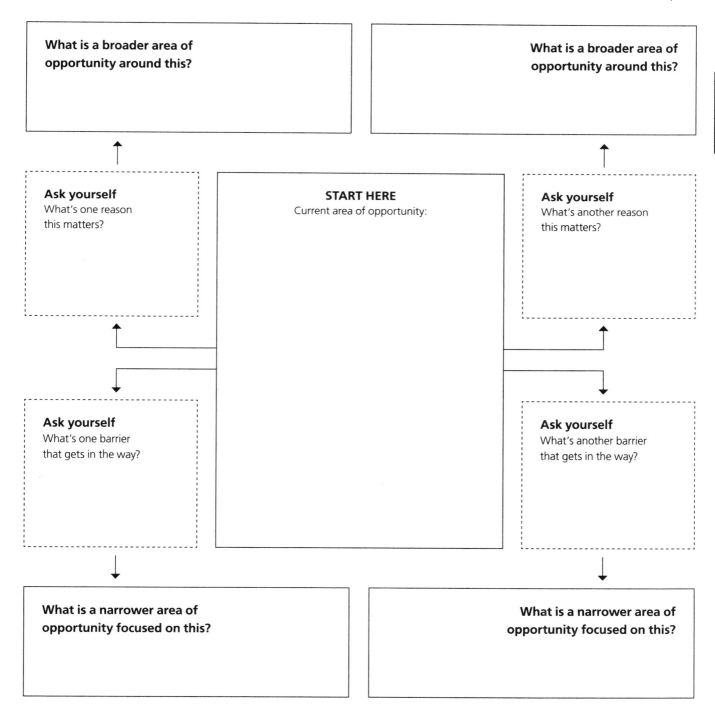

What is a broader area of opportunity around this?

What is a broader area of opportunity around this?

Ask yourself
What's one reason this matters?

START HERE
Current area of opportunity:

Ask yourself
What's another reason this matters?

Ask yourself
What's one barrier that gets in the way?

Ask yourself
What's another barrier that gets in the way?

What is a narrower area of opportunity focused on this?

What is a narrower area of opportunity focused on this?

STEPS

Step 3: Draft Your Design Brief

A well-constructed project process is rooted in a design brief that clarifies the scope of the project, its intent, the questions it hopes to explore, and the target group of stakeholders—internal and external—that it wants to explore them with. The design brief keeps you focused on your business objectives and the strategic opportunities and vulnerabilities your project is meant to address.

We spend time carefully thinking through our plans and ambitions because even though our environment is full of uncertainty, the management of our design project doesn't need to be. Since some key elements of the design process are uncontrollable, it is all the more important to drive ambiguity out of the management of the project itself. That is the role of your design brief—to help you get as much clarity, control, and transparency into the management of your project as possible. It should also be useful for keeping important stakeholders (your boss, your partners, etc.) informed.

The design brief should be limited to two pages so that it is concise and simple to update as the project moves ahead. Here is a template you can use.

As we move forward, we want to keep in mind that the design brief is always a work in progress that may change as our understanding of the problem evolves.

Jot your notes here:

See D4G pages 44-46 for additional detail and examples.

Design Brief

Project Description	What is the problem or opportunity? Describe the project in a few sentences, as you would in an "elevator pitch."
Scope	What is within the scope of the project and what is outside it? What efforts sit adjacent to this particular project?
Constraints	What constraints do you need to work within? What requirements must a successful solution meet?
Target Users	Who are you designing for? Try to be as specific as possible. Whom do you need to understand? Why are they important?
Exploration Questions	What key questions will you need to answer through your research? What are you curious to learn about your stakeholders and how they think and behave? These may include stakeholder needs to understand better, emerging technical possibilities and new business models.
Expected Outcomes	What outcomes would you like to see?
Success Metrics	How will you measure success?

Step 4: Make Your Plans

Every challenge is different, so take some time to develop a plan that's custom-made for your challenge. Think about your time frame. Consider what tools you might use. (Hint: There's a great planning guide on the facing page.) Will you work alone or with others? (Hint: The more the merrier, especially when exploring **What is** and **What *if***) Where will you work? (Hint: A "war room" or other location where you can hang posters helps.) When will you get started? **The sooner the better!**

There are three different elements you will want to consider explicitly: activities (what tools you will use and what you will do), people (the stakeholders and supporters you'll rely on), and research (how you'll gather data to inform your work). Let's look at each in turn.

Jot your notes here:

Your Project Plan

How will you approach your journey through the four questions? Take some time to investigate what tools to use and the order in which you'll use them. We suggest that you read ahead now and review the upcoming steps to familiarize yourself with the array of available tools before making your choices below.

Before you begin

☐ Step 1: Identify an Opportunity
☐ Step 2: Scope Your Project
☐ Step 3: Draft Your Design Brief
☐ Step 4: Make Your Plans
 (you are here)

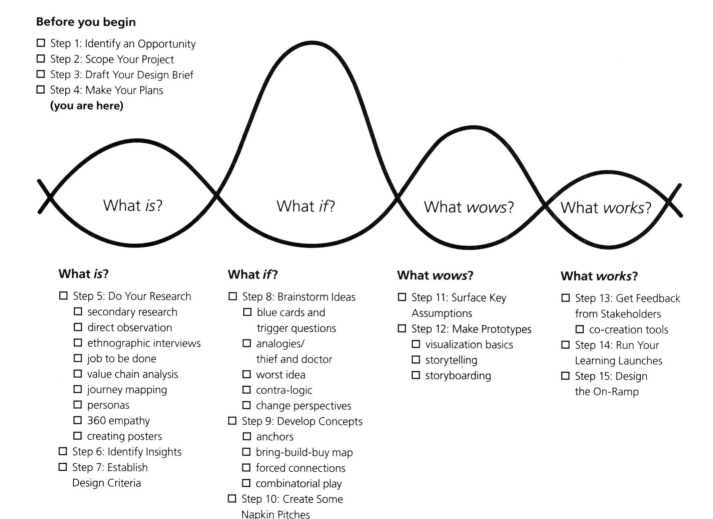

What *is*?   What *if*?   What *wows*?   What *works*?

What *is*?

☐ Step 5: Do Your Research
  ☐ secondary research
  ☐ direct observation
  ☐ ethnographic interviews
  ☐ job to be done
  ☐ value chain analysis
  ☐ journey mapping
  ☐ personas
  ☐ 360 empathy
  ☐ creating posters
☐ Step 6: Identify Insights
☐ Step 7: Establish
 Design Criteria

What *if*?

☐ Step 8: Brainstorm Ideas
  ☐ blue cards and
   trigger questions
  ☐ analogies/
   thief and doctor
  ☐ worst idea
  ☐ contra-logic
  ☐ change perspectives
☐ Step 9: Develop Concepts
  ☐ anchors
  ☐ bring-build-buy map
  ☐ forced connections
  ☐ combinatorial play
☐ Step 10: Create Some
 Napkin Pitches

What *wows*?

☐ Step 11: Surface Key
 Assumptions
☐ Step 12: Make Prototypes
  ☐ visualization basics
  ☐ storytelling
  ☐ storyboarding

What *works*?

☐ Step 13: Get Feedback
 from Stakeholders
  ☐ co-creation tools
☐ Step 14: Run Your
 Learning Launches
☐ Step 15: Design
 the On-Ramp

Your People Plan

Now it's time to think about the human beings who are the target of your efforts or whose help you need in order to succeed. Think about the whole range of people your project might impact—customers (internal and external), colleagues, partners, decision makers, thought leaders, competitors. List them here.

Who is already in your network? What's the status of your relationship? Who's not in your network? Where will you locate them? What's your strategy for engaging the ones most critical to your success?

One key when approaching a project full of ambiguity is to take the time to consider people as the complex, multi-faceted creatures they are, complete with needs and wants and motivations. Not only will your efforts help you build alignment and support, they might also provide insights and clues to opportunities that await. Think about a few of the most important stakeholders—customers, colleagues, partners—whose cooperation you need and ask yourself the following questions:

Stakeholder/User #1 Name _____	Stakeholder/User #2 Name _____	Stakeholder/User #3 Name _____
What is their current point of view? How will their behavior or actions need to be different in order to address my challenge?	What is their current point of view? How will their behavior or actions need to be different in order to address my challenge?	What is their current point of view? How will their behavior or actions need to be different in order to address my challenge?
What am I curious about related to this stakeholder?	What am I curious about related to this stakeholder?	What am I curious about related to this stakeholder?
How can I develop empathy for this stakeholder?	How can I develop empathy for this stakeholder?	How can I develop empathy for this stakeholder?

Your Research Plan

When it comes to design thinking, our inspiration comes from data. But it's not simply data that we've grown accustomed to from reading financial reports and studying compiled survey data. Instead, we're looking for data on a very human scale—individual stories about people and their needs and how they relate to your opportunity.

Take a moment to think about whom you might need to interview or observe in order to gather this kind of human-centered data. Later on in the field book, you'll explore a few different approaches to help you gather the information and make sense of it. In the meantime, use this space to begin your research plan. You can always come back later to add to or adjust it.

Who or what will we study?	Where will we find the people or information?	What questions/issues will we explore?	Number of observations, interviews, or inputs	When will the research happen?	Who on the team is responsible?

Step 5: Do Your Research

OK. You've made your plans. Now it's time to dive in and begin exploring **What *is.***

First you're going to gather some data. Here you have some choices, which you considered when developing your research plan as part of Step 4. Take time to review these again, using the list of tools in the back of this field book.

To familiarize yourself and get the lay of the land—as well as to begin to identify some of the major trends that might be impacting your project and the opportunity—you might want to begin with **secondary research** (page 44).

Just like scientists and bird-watchers like to view their specimens in a natural habitat, we often get our first clues about the real opportunities related to our project when we watch users do what they're already doing. Check out **direct observation** (page 46) for some tips on how to get started.

Since we can't actually crawl around inside people's heads, we need another way to find about what they're thinking. Learn how to ask questions that solicit hidden information about attitudes, beliefs, and needs by turning to **ethnographic interviews** (page 48).

Often we find that despite the best-laid plans, a project can start to fizzle here. Maybe it's difficult to secure the time or resources to execute your research plan, or you're having a hard time finding the courage to get out there and talk to some real customers. If you get stuck, return to your people plan and consider how your network can help unstick you. You'll be glad you did.

See D4G pages 61-80 for additional detail and examples.

A sea of data is only as good as what you can learn from it, so a good design thinker takes time to look for patterns and insights in the mountains of notes. Unlike tabulating quantitative surveys, this kind of "sense-making" involves play and experimentation as you work to sort all the information you've collected.

Here are some tips for choosing among the tools in the back of this field book for processing and organizing the data you've gathered. Go ahead and take note of the tools that you'd like to use, and then flip to their respective pages to read more. We think it's a good idea to choose at least two of these approaches.

If you're trying to pinpoint your stakeholders' unmet needs, then the **job to be done** tool is a great way to explore this more deeply. Turn to page 50.

If you want to look at how a community of suppliers comes together to create value—and where there might be opportunity for more—then the **value chain analysis** tool is for you. Turn to page 52.

If the opportunity you're seeking has to do with a process or a sequence of activities, then **journey mapping** is a great way to guide and synthesize your ethnographic interviews. Turn to page 54. We highly recommend a journey map for every design thinking project that involves a process or a purchase decision.

If you're trying to understand how to refine your target stakeholder groups, then the **personas** tool is a great way to home in on more-segmented needs. Turn to page 56. After that, create an even richer portrait of your end user with the **360 empathy** tool on page 58.

Step 6: Identify Insights

Now it is time to look for patterns and insights in the large quantity of data you've collected during your exploration of **What** *is.* The goal here is to establish the criteria for the **What** *if* idea generation stage, which comes next. You move to this step when you feel like you have collected representative data from each relevant stakeholder group—colleagues, customers, suppliers, partners, and your own operations—and are eager to begin generating new ideas. For many people, identifying insights is the most difficult part of the design process. Usually, you cannot expect a stakeholder to come up with a deep insight and hand it to you. Insights emerge as you pore over the information you've gathered, looking for patterns.

In our experience, structuring a team process for the identification of insights, which we call mind mapping, is especially helpful. Not only are you going deep into the data you've collected to define the criteria for an ideal solution for your target stakeholders, you are also aligning team members' view of **What** *is*—you are creating a common mind.

Bonus: After identifying your insights, cycle back to your design brief to see if you can better reframe the opportunity even more through the lens of the user.

Every firm is reading the market data and trying to come up with new ideas. Novelty doesn't drive growth, however. Solving an unmet user need does. So you want your insights to come together in a way that fundamentally reframes the opportunity. A good reframing helps your team see possibilities that were always there but were hidden from view.

A team at the pharmaceutical company Pfizer exploring opportunities for a smoking cessation offering found that smokers ages 25 to 35 don't think of their habit as a medical issue or an addiction; they view it as a temporary lifestyle choice. So, the team reframed smoking cessation in this way:

Initial Frame:
"Help me overcome my chemical addiction"

Reframe:
"Support me as I make a new lifestyle choice"

Use your insights to form a reframe that connects to a hidden truth about what users want, and your concepts can breathe new life into an established category.

See D4G pages 87 and 91 for additional detail and examples.

Here is the process we recommend:

1. **Create large visuals of your learnings and put them up on the walls for everyone to see—like an art gallery.** (We recommend using the **creating posters** tool on page 60.) Chances are you already have some customer journey maps, persona 2x2s, and value chains to display. Put your posters up all over the walls, along with any other data that you want your team to know about.

2. **Ask members to browse individually (without talking to one another) and note data in the gallery that they believe should inform your thinking.** Ask people to write one piece of data per Post-it note, being sure to write specifics from each of the posters rather than interpretations. Ask them to write legibly in block letters that everyone can read. Encourage them to avoid writing down a single word—look for phrases that will mean something to other team members when they read them.

3. **Cluster all the data you've gathered using a two-step process.** Have each team member spend five minutes privately sorting through their Post-its and clustering them into piles of related information. After completing this, the team should work as a group to cluster members' combined Post-its into a shared mind map. We suggest using a specific process like this:

- One team member starts by sharing one of his or her Post-it notes, reading it aloud, and sticking it on a shared board.

- One at a time, other team members then contribute any of their individual Post-it notes, also reading aloud, that relate to the same topic.

- A second team member then starts a new cluster and the process continues until all Post-it notes have been added to the shared mind map.

4. **Work together to identify the insights related to each cluster.** This can be challenging. It helps to start by labeling each cluster—what is it about? (For example, a cluster might be about "technology.") Then push harder to transform these labels into "so what" themes (such as "Technology makes it harder for people to do their jobs"). Sometimes you may find that you have more than one insight per cluster, especially when the Post-its in that cluster are telling you different things. These insights should be written on larger Post-its and placed on top of the relevant cluster.

Step 7: Establish Design Criteria

The result of your mind mapping is the creation of a set of design criteria, a succinct expression of the ideal end state of your project. They describe the ideal qualities or attributes of a great solution, but not the solution itself. That part comes next, during **What** *if.*

This translation process is usually pretty straightforward. If your insight was "Technology makes it hard for people to do their job," your design criteria for an ideal solution might be "uses technology that helps people do their jobs" or "only utilizes technology that doesn't get in the way."

Taking each individual insight you identified in Step 6, translate it into a criterion for your ideal solution by asking yourself the following: *"If anything were possible, our ideal solution would … "*

When complete, your list of criteria should encompass user needs and perceptions, physical parameters, functional requirements, and core constraints. In most cases, you'll want a list of six to eight criteria.

Jot your notes here:

See D4G pages 97-100 for additional detail and examples.

Here are some questions that may help in ensuring that your listing of criteria doesn't miss anything important:

Design Criteria

Design Goal	What needs (functional, emotional, psychological, social) does the design have to fulfill for the stakeholder? Why is it strategically important for your organization to address those needs?
User Perceptions	Are there aesthetic attributes necessary to succeed with the target stakeholder? Does the target stakeholder expect the offering to have certain social, ethical, or ecological attributes? What does ease-of-use mean to the target stakeholder?
Physical Attributes	Does the offering need to be designed for use in specific environments or situations? Are there weight or size considerations for lifting, use, or transport? Must the offering be able to capture, store, and/or transmit information about usage?
Functional Attributes	Does the design of the offering need to accommodate specific situations or occasions? Does the design need to address compatibility or standards issues? Existing processes or procedures?
Constraints	Does the final offering need to be completed by a specific date? Within a defined budget? What constraints does your current business impose (e.g., use of existing manufacturing base)? Are there ecosystem and/or regulatory concerns (e.g., the height of shelves at retailers)?

Step 8: Brainstorm Ideas

Finally — time to generate solutions!

We've all had experiences in brainstorming sessions that were, well, less than inspiring. In fact, we find that brainstorming has a pretty bad reputation. Regardless, design thinking requires the deliberate generation of a lot—a whole lot—of possibilities. Here are some tips to fuel your brainstorming efforts.

- **Assemble a diverse set of people.** Success in brainstorming comes from using small, diverse groups, as free as possible from internal political considerations. Brainstorming cannot abide groupthink, so it is essential to go way beyond the project's core team.

- **Work with a clearly stated challenge.** The brainstorming team must focus on a clearly stated challenge. The design criteria represent a great starting point.

- **Encourage the right mind-set.** The mind-set you need for brainstorming is that of the creator, not the critic. Some rules:

  - One voice at a time
  - No filibusters (30 seconds per idea)
  - Show your work (sketches and stick figures)
  - Withhold judgment (evaluation occurs later)
  - Build on the ideas of others
  - Have fun!

- **Inspire people.** People are inspired by people. It's as simple as that. For a successful brainstorming session, participants must care about the problem, and that means that you must show them its human costs. Here is where the fieldwork you completed in the **What *is*** stage can come in handy. Use it to create a persona of a stakeholder who experiences the problem you are focused on.

- **Select your brainstorming tool.** Turn to pages 62-67 and select at least two brainstorming techniques that you want to use. Then jot some notes about possible trigger questions or analogies or elements of contra-logic you want to include.

See D4G pages 103-110 for additional detail and examples.

Creating great trigger questions can be the key to brainstorming success. Here's a little "formula" we have found useful:

Question 1:

Make it wide open to cover the entire breadth of the opportunity. Use this to surface the ideas people have been holding on to since the beginning and to draw momentum from the highlights of the **What is** findings.

Example:
"How could we improve the accounts payable process?"

Bonus Question: Reduce the risk threshold and inject some fun by soliciting bad ideas. We like to use this immediately after question 1 because it sets a good tone for the remaining questions, but it can be held until later in the sequence.

Question 2:

Focus on one or two specific elements of the design criteria that are closely linked to the user needs identified in the research. As time and interest allow, you might use multiple questions here and extend the session, with each question focusing on a different element of the criteria. Use simple, broad language in the question.

Example:
"How could we ensure that everyone understands the accounts payable process from beginning to end?"

Question 3:

Draw on a metaphor or analogy. Identify a situation analogous to an aspect of the opportunity (use the analogies tool on page 65 to help with this) and use that to inspire the group's thinking.

Example:
"Imagine that our data analytics tools are the librarians of information. What practices of traditional and digital libraries could we adapt and adopt?"

Step 9: Develop Concepts

Concept development is the act of choosing the best ideas from brainstorming and assembling them into an array of detailed solutions. You want to build multiple concepts so that you can offer a choice to your primary audience, your stakeholder. Think of your ideas as individual Legos—it is time to build some cool creations by combining them in different ways.

Most of us are accustomed to concluding a brainstorming session by selecting our favorite ideas from among the sea of Post-it notes. This is like a chef who takes all the best vegetables from the farmers' market and dumps them all together in a pot without selecting combinations that work together, then washing, slicing, dicing, and seasoning those ingredients.

You want to get the most from your ideas, and to do that, we need to do a little prep work. The tools section in the back of this field book includes four methods for developing concepts. Choose one or try all four.

If you notice some big themes brewing amidst all the brainstormed ideas, the **anchors** tool is a great way to take a few ideas from lukewarm to sizzling by playing up key dimensions. Turn to page 68.

To highlight how your firm might actually produce and deliver the new concept, complete the **bring-build-buy** map. Turn to page 70.

To use serendipity to stretch your thinking, practice exercising your concept development muscle with the **forced connections** tool. Turn to page 72.

Finally, to ensure you've systematically explored a wide variety of possibilities, turn to an explanation of **combinatorial play** on page 74.

See D4G pages 113-117 for additional detail and examples.

Capture some of the concepts that spark your imagination here.

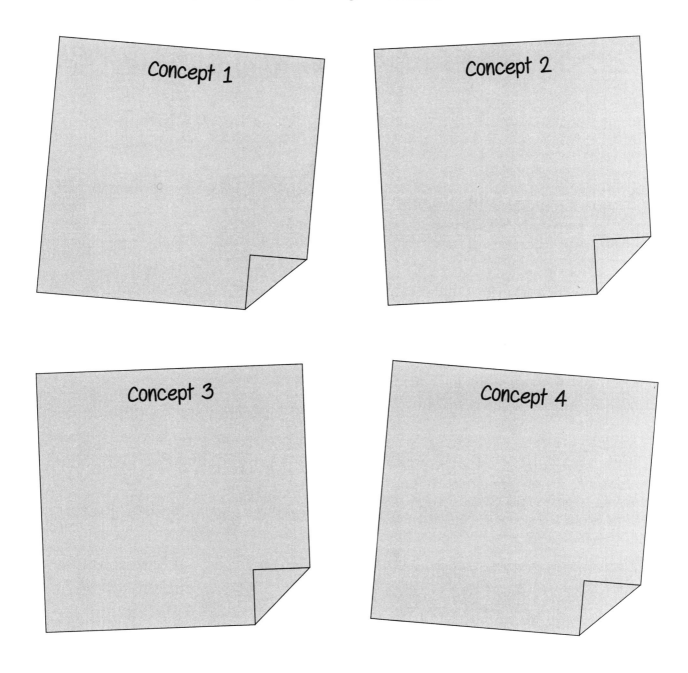

Step 10: Create Some Napkin Pitches

The napkin pitch provides a simple, consistent format for summarizing and communicating new concepts. The name derives from the notion that a good idea can (and should) be communicated simply—so simply that it would fit on the back of a napkin. Because napkins tend to jam printer trays, we've translated the concept into a one-page template that might not be useful for wiping your hands but will do a great job of letting you and your team work on multiple innovation concepts in parallel.

For a given concept, the napkin pitch describes the target stakeholders, their unmet need, and why your offering creates novel value for them; the elements you will make, buy, and partner for; the channels you will use; and the potential rivals or other factors to watch.

Use the napkin pitch at the conclusion of concept development, to summarize the short list of concepts coming out of **What *if*** that you want to explore further in the **What *wows*** stage. You should have at least three napkin pitches developed before you move forward; it's not unusual for practiced design thinkers to want to explore a dozen napkin pitches further.

See D4G pages 124-126 for additional detail and examples.

Take one of your concepts and lay it out here.

Napkin Pitch

CONCEPT NAME:

The Big Idea Describe the concept.	**Needs/Benefits** What stakeholder wants this? What unmet needs does it serve? How will the stakeholder benefit?
Execution How will we deliver? What asset or capability does this leverage or require? What partners do we need?	**Business Rationale** How will this address the opportunity defined in our design brief? What makes us uniquely capable of delivering this? How will our competition react? How will we sustain our advantage?

Step 11: Surface Key Assumptions

Before we start bringing a napkin pitch to life, we need to surface the key assumptions underlying the attractiveness of a concept and to use data to assess the likelihood that these assumptions are true. This approach acknowledges that any business concept is actually a hypothesis—a well-informed guess about what stakeholders want and what they will value. Like any hypothesis, a new business concept is built on assumptions that must be valid in order for the hypothesis to be "true," so testing them is essential. Projects fail because reality turns out to be different than you thought it would be. Launching new concepts to see if they work in the real world is a risky and potentially expensive approach that you want to avoid for all but the most attractive ones. Minimize risk and expenditure by rolling out only those concepts that pass a set of initial thought tests around value creation, execution, scalability, and defensibility.

Write Down All Key Assumptions. Use the four tests (the row headings) on the next page to help define the key assumptions for your concept. Identify the top two or three assumptions in each category.

Set a Test Strategy. Different assumptions need to be tested using different approaches, and in order of importance. Always use the lowest-cost, lowest-risk approach to get the job done, starting with your most critical assumptions.

1. **Thought Experiments:** For some assumptions, you may already have useful data you can use.

2. **2D & 3D Simulation Experiments:** For assumptions where no source of data exists, do a quick co-creation session with stakeholders using low-fidelity prototypes.

3. **Live (4D) In-Market Experiments:** Some assumptions, especially those based on consumer behavior, will require a live, in-market experiment.

Revisit and Refine. The key assumptions will become a reference point for the rest of the project. You'll want to revisit them after Step 13 (Feedback) and Step 14 (Learning Launches), in particular.

See D4G pages 131-138 for additional detail and examples.

Key Assumptions

CONCEPT NAME:		TE	2D/3D	4D
VALUE TEST • Customers want it • Customers will pay for it • Partners want it				
EXECUTION TEST • We can produce the experience technically • We can acquire customers • We can operate the business as it grows				
SCALE TEST • Addressable market is big enough • We can acquire customers affordably • Revenues exceed costs at scale				
DEFENSIBILITY TEST • We can protect advantage • Advantage increases as we grow the business				

STEPS

THOUGHT EXPERIMENT

- Learn through analysis of existing data
- Typical time frame: one or two days
- No exposure to third parties required

2D & 3D SIMULATION EXPERIMENT

- Learn through dialog with market participants using storyboards or prototypes
- Typical time frame: one or two weeks
- May require us to expose our intentions to selected market participants

LIVE (4D) IN-MARKET EXPERIMENT

- Test via a live experience of the offering (e.g., a 30-day live trial)
- Typical time frame: 30 to 90 days
- Requires us to expose our offering to many market participants

Step 12: Make Prototypes

Rapid prototyping is the creation of visual (and sometimes experiential) manifestations of concepts. It is an iterative set of activities, done quickly, aimed at transforming the concepts generated in the **What *if*** stage into feasible, testable models. You build prototypes as the next step in the assumption testing process. In prototyping, you're giving your concepts detail, form, and nuance—you bring them to life. Larry Keeley, of Doblin, an innovation consultancy, calls prototyping "faking a new business fast."

The first role of a prototype is to help us figure out **what** to build. Only later, after users have interacted with many iterations of the "what to build" prototype, will we create refined prototypes that help us figure out **how** to build it.

It is easy to prototype a new toothbrush, and harder to prototype a business process or experience. Early prototypes are necessarily crude and unfinished in appearance—they look like incomplete works in progress. But the incompleteness is good—it invites users to interact with and improve upon the prototype.

Whatever format you find appropriate, be sure it features people. (You know—actual human beings with thoughts and feelings and personalities.) Too often we jump to technical wiring diagrams and process flows that are almost meaningless to prospective users. The prototype needs to tell a story and elicit an emotional response—and to invite the end user to shape the final solution.

2D prototypes come in many forms

- Flowcharts convey the basic building blocks of a new experience

- Storyboards move beyond a functional view and into the human story of an experience, shifting the focus to the user and the need that the new experience fills in her life

- Metaphorical prototypes elicit a gut reaction and promote a dialog with a target user, without doing any selling of specific features or benefits

- Videos allow you to create the appearance of the service without actually building it

- Interactive building blocks are all about enlisting users physically in the design of a new experience and can use a variety of approaches, from mix-and-match drawings to simple digital models

- Business concept illustrations express a new experience from multiple perspectives, including the user experience, the technology, and the business model

See D4G pages 141-147 for additional detail and examples.

Use this space to consider a 2D prototype of one of your napkin pitch concepts. Emphasize images over words. Be sure to give people (customers or users) a prominent role in the schematic or storyboard.

Step 13: Get Feedback from Stakeholders

Stakeholder or customer co-creation is the process of engaging potential stakeholders/customers in the development of new concepts. It involves putting some rough prototypes in front of them, observing their reactions, and using the results to iterate your way to an improved concept. If you want your innovations to be meaningful to those you are trying to create value for, you need to invite them into your process.

In our Six Sigma world, which values perfection and polish, we tend to get anxious about showing stakeholders unfinished, unpolished "stuff." But innovation is about learning—and stakeholders/customers have the most to teach you. The sooner you get something in front of them that they can react to, the faster you'll get to a differentiated value-added solution. And they will love being involved.

1. **Enroll stakeholders who care about you (but not as much as they care about themselves).** You need stakeholders/customers whom you trust (since they are being exposed to your possible future plans) and who are hungry for a solution and motivated to be completely candid.

2. **Diversity = security.** Enroll a diverse group of stakeholders/customers for co-creation sessions. There is a temptation to choose only target stakeholders/customers, but you may be surprised to learn that non-targets are just as keen for what you have to offer.

3. **Create a no-selling zone.** Co-creation sessions are not opportunities to "sell" your solution. A rule of thumb is that the stakeholder/customer should do at least 80% of the talking. You want candid feedback, not false agreement.

4. **Engage one stakeholder/customer at a time.** This may seem inefficient—but remember that you are not going for a statistically significant sample size. You will learn so much more from them when there is no social pressure—when they are alone with you and not influenced by others expressing their opinions at the same time.

5. **Offer a small menu of choices.** Presenting a single concept, well considered, defies the purpose of co-creation. Typically, you want to give stakeholders/customers two or three options and invite them to begin exploring one that they are drawn to.

See D4G pages 159-165 for additional detail and examples.

A typical co-creation phase might have three rounds, each reflecting the changes and improvements learned in the previous rounds. There are a variety of prototypes that can be used during customer co-creation, but one of the most basic (and most effective) formats is the concept storyboard and discussion guide.

Along with the concept storyboard, you should also write a series of questions and probes around each story panel to elicit feedback from customers in your co-creation session. These questions will be your discussion guide and will help you stay focused on the key assumptions and concept features you most want to understand.

Once a customer/stakeholder has modified the storyboard, take a photo of the changes, then reset it to its beginning form. Now you're ready for the next co-creation session.

When debriefing your co-creation session later, use these topics to help you capture all of your impressions:

- **Stimulus:** What you showed users to gauge their response
- **Observation:** What they did and said (literal transcript)
- **Feelings:** What emotions their response signaled to you
- **Needs:** The underlying needs that may be indicated by those emotions
- **Implications:** What this means for us

Step 14: Run Your Learning Launches

Learning launches are experiments conducted in the real world quickly and inexpensively. They form a bridge between co-creation and a rollout. In contrast to a full new-product rollout, a learning launch's success is about not how much you sell but how much you learn. The goal of each launch is to test some of the remaining critical assumptions (which you surfaced in Step 11) about why this is an attractive concept.

Use the learning launch tool when you are ready to ask stakeholders to put some skin in the game. Merely asking what they think, however useful for developing a new concept, is a weak form of testing it. Unlike a co-creation session, learning launches need to feel real to both launchers and stakeholders. And unlike a pilot, a learning launch needs to be tightly constrained during execution but open to major changes at the end.

Once you have a prototype, a goal, and a time frame, the skills you already have for project management will get you most of the way there, along with these success principles:

1. **Set tight boundaries.** Since this is a learning launch and not a pilot, it is important to plan for it to end. Set concrete limits on key variables, such as time, geography, number of stakeholders, features, and partners.

2. **Design with a sharp focus on the key assumptions that need to be tested.** Pay special attention to "make or break" assumptions and areas where you can learn quickly and cheaply.

3. **Be explicit about how you will generate the data you need, especially behavioral data.** Also be explicit about the search for disconfirming data.

4. **Build a team that is both disciplined and adaptive.** Have a few skeptics around to ensure that you aren't designing a test to give you the answers you want. Conducting a learning launch is a team sport, and the composition of the team makes a difference.

5. **Think fast and cheap.** The learning launch is when your project first makes contact with reality. Expect surprises, and be prepared to respond quickly.

6. **Make it feel real.** Everyone has something at stake. If your test feels like a game of make-believe, then the behavioral data it generates are suspect.

7. **Consider a series of learning launches.** Once you gather data to test your initial assumptions, review where you are and move on to another round. (Or, in the event that your concept hasn't met some "make or break" criteria, table this concept for another day.)

See D4G pages 167-177 for additional detail and examples.

Your learning launch design should be specific. Make sure you articulate all the basics:

- **Who** is the target stakeholder of this test? (actual names are best. If you don't have them, describe how you'll get actual people to participate.)
- **Where** will you conduct the test?

- **How** will you test this element of your napkin pitch and make it feel real?
- **Cost** What is your budget for the learning launch?
- **Time** What's your timetable?

Learning Launch Design	
Key Assumptions to Test	**Learning Launch # _____**
	Who
	Where
	How
	Cost
	Time

After you design your learning launch (but before you actually conduct it), make note of what data would validate or disprove each assumption you're testing. This helps make sure you don't misinterpret your findings.

What to Watch For		
Untested Assumptions	**Success Metric**	**Disconfirming Data**

Step 15: Design the On-Ramp

When you design your new experience, you naturally will be obsessed with how the experience works when customers use it. But you also have to ask yourself, "How will those users get here in the first place?" That is, how do customers learn about the offering, try it out, become regular users, and enlist others?

Think of this as the on-ramp. To simply call it the customer acquisition strategy is to risk demoting it to a page in a PowerPoint deck. Instead, the on-ramp must be brainstormed, prototyped, co-created, and iterated just as carefully as the solution it serves. (And don't fall prey to thinking that on-ramps apply only to consumer products; they're equally relevant and important when considering the adoption of new systems, procedures, and services.)

Think of the on-ramp as a ladder that leads your target user to become a zealous advocate. Your focus prior to this step in the design thinking process has been on #5 and #6 in the figure below. To design the on-ramp, you must shift your attention to #1 through #4. With this in mind:

1. Hold a brainstorming session focused exclusively on possible on-ramps.

2. Use the tips shown on these pages to think it through.

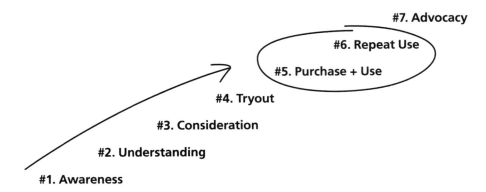

#7. Advocacy

#6. Repeat Use

#5. Purchase + Use

#4. Tryout

#3. Consideration

#2. Understanding

#1. Awareness

See D4G page 174 for additional detail and examples.

Tips for Effective On-Ramps

Use artifacts. If you want bystanders to notice the solution, you need to provide an intriguing artifact that gets noticed. Amazon makes its logo prominent on its box because many orders are shipped to the workplace, where others will see the packages.

Build in network value. Design your service so users will find it valuable to connect with others. Online photo services enable sharing, which provides a crucial on-ramp for new customers.

Enable user-created content. Let people customize their own content. LinkedIn and other network services depend heavily on getting people to share their created content with others as an on-ramp.

Provide social capital. If you give social recognition to power users, it will make others want to emulate them. The airline frequent flyer programs turn their top flyers into ambassadors this way. Ebay designates "power sellers." These mechanisms are highly affordable on-ramps.

Provide social pressure. Social pressure works just as social capital does. If you want all your employees who are smokers to sign up for a smoking cessation program, send an enrollment postcard to their home address so their spouses will see the offer and encourage (i.e., pressure) them to sign up.

Use affordable giveaways. It may be necessary to nudge prospective users up the on-ramp through giveaways. Starbucks often gives "$2 off" coupons for any cold beverage after 2PM. This is the on-ramp to help customers add an afternoon visit on top of their morning visit.

Pre-sell through social media. Often, we can explore on-ramps even before we've created a 3D prototype, simply by advertising an early version of the solution in social media. Buy some Google AdWords or embark on a LinkedIn campaign to enlist alpha testers once the solution is ready. You can easily discover the potential for online on-ramps this way.

Test alternative on-ramps. During the learning launch, try out different on-ramp approaches to see which ones work best.

Write down some possible on-ramp elements for your concept(s) here.

STEPS

What Now? What Next?

At this point you might ask, "What's next?" If your learning launch results suggest the concept is unlikely to succeed, you may decide to table this challenge and shift your attention to a more promising opportunity.

If, on the other hand, you and your team are encouraged by the results of the learning launch, then it's time to iterate. You'll want to:

- Brainstorm solutions to the parts that failed during the learning launch (Step 8)
- Revise your concept and napkin pitch (Steps 9 and 10)
- Refine your key assumptions (Step 11)
- Create a higher-fidelity prototype (Step 12)
- Develop ways to engage customers in co-creation (Step 13)
- Execute another learning launch (Step 14)
- Explore alternative on-ramps (Step 15)

As you can see, steps 8 through 15 in this field book represent a learning loop. As we develop more confidence in each concept, we refine the elements and home in on a path to commercialization or implementation. Each loop represents an affordable investment to get to the next threshold of understanding about the opportunity. This is how design thinking manages risk—through action in the market instead of analytics.

A typical set of learning loops (or iterations) might look like this:

Experiment Description	Time Span	Expenses
2D paper prototype *90-minute co-creation sessions with 12 target users*	2 weeks	$500
3D digital storyboard *90-minute co-creation sessions with 12 target users*	6 weeks	$5,000
4D alpha test *Based on a working prototype (non-scalable back end)* *Operate solution for 1 month with 20-50 live users*	10 weeks	$50,000
Beta test *Working version of the first feature set, based on a scalable back end* *Operate solution for 3 months with 100-500 live users*	20 weeks	$250,000

Congratulations! You've navigated the four questions of the design thinking process. Take some time to reflect on what you've learned—about yourself and about these methods for navigating complex challenges and practicing breakthrough thinking.

What tools did you use?

Which tools or steps were aha! moments?

Which activities seemed to foster collaboration?

What other challenges are you facing—personally or as a leader in your organization—that might be addressed using these tools? Where do you want to turn your attention next?

The Tools

Secondary Research

TOOL FOR STEP 5 (p. 16)

Don't forget what you already know (or what other people have already found out). Gather the data you have, and use industry experts, associations, and thought leaders to fill in the gaps. There's a lot out there.

Direct Observation

TOOL FOR STEP 5 (p. 16)

Sometimes the only way to know what's going on is to see it with your own eyes. Make sure you know what you're getting into. Identify your end user, find out where he or she is, and put on your virtual binoculars.

Ethnographic Interviews

TOOL FOR STEP 5 (p. 16)

Dig beneath the surface with this anthropological interviewing technique to elicit your user's back story and find out more about what happens between the ears. It's not like any other interview you've done.

Job to Be Done

TOOL FOR STEP 5 (p. 16)

Unmet needs can be tricky, since they're often buried deep beneath a stakeholder's presenting concern. Take a look at the reason people do the things they do. You might be surprised by what you discover.

Value Chain Analysis

TOOL FOR STEP 5 (p. 16)

Hunt for sources of real value. Here, you'll study your interaction with suppliers and partners to create and deliver your offering. By looking at your internal processes and capabilities, you'll get clues to opportunities.

Journey Mapping

TOOL FOR STEP 5 (p. 16)

If the opportunity you're seeking has to do with a process or a sequence of activities, then journey mapping is a great way to synthesize your interviews. Look for opportunities to enhance your stakeholders' journeys.

Personas

TOOL FOR STEP 5 (p. 16)

At this stage, we don't care much about traditional market segmentation, but we do want to understand the key drivers of all the potential users out there. Use this tool to find commonalities (and differences) that matter.

360 Empathy

TOOL FOR STEP 5 (p. 16)

Take a persona to the next level with 360 empathy. Use this tool to put yourself in the place of your user and see the opportunity with your user's senses. It's a launching pad to bring your user to life and meet real needs.

Creating Posters

TOOL FOR STEP 5 (p. 16)

Once you've assembled your data from **What is,** it's time to share what you've learned. Resist the habit of opening up the presentation software on your computer. Instead, use these tips to create posters that spark new conversations.

Brainstorming

TOOL FOR STEP 8 (p. 22)

Step away from the blank whiteboard. Make sure that your brainstorming doesn't just lead to all the ideas you've generated before. Use metaphor and triggers to get started. Want extra credit? Try two methods.

Anchors

TOOL FOR STEP 9 (p. 24)

Build on the themes in your ideas. Just as an anchor keeps the cruise ship in port, an anchor helps your emerging concept stay grounded in all those insights you gathered earlier in the process. It's a great way to expand on an idea.

Bring-Build-Buy Map

TOOL FOR STEP 9 (p. 24)

Set out the possible building blocks for your supply chain by completing this analysis. Think of it as a make-buy template with unmet needs as the North Star.

Forced Connections

TOOL FOR STEP 9 (p. 24)

Put your creative muscle to work with this tool to stretch your thinking. Get a group of people together (four to six is good) and play with the ideas you generated. The zanier the initial combination, the better.

Combinatorial Play

TOOL FOR STEP 9 (p. 24)

Use your brainstormed ideas as building blocks in this systematic approach to mix-and-match. This is a great tool for ensuring that you don't miss any opportunity, no matter how unconventional or surprising.

Visualization Basics

TOOL FOR STEP 12 (p. 30)

They say a picture's worth a thousand words. They underestimate. Don't let a lack of artistic skill keep you from putting visualization to work for you. Turn here for simple ways to help pictures work for you.

Storytelling

TOOL FOR STEP 12 (p. 30)

Most of the time when we explain a napkin pitch, we focus on what we are going to do. A simple formula for stories flips the focus to help us explore the potential from our user's point of view. Once upon a time …

Storyboarding

TOOL FOR STEP 12 (p. 30)

It's not just something they do for the movies. Storyboarding is a form of 2D prototype that helps show your concept in action simply and cheaply. It tells a story, so it's great for putting your user right into the picture.

Co-Creation Tools

TOOL FOR STEP 13 (p. 32)

It's hard to partner with your user without sliding into "sell" mode. These tools can help make sure that your conversations stay firmly grounded in exploration and iteration. They also make them more fun.

Secondary Research

Just because you are using design thinking and incorporating ethnography, it doesn't mean you should ignore the quantitative or qualitative data you've already got. Past research reports, user surveys, performance data, and financial reports can all be important additions to your **What *is*** gallery. Not only do they contribute to a richer picture of current reality, but including this information may also be reassuring to any of your colleagues who are a touch skeptical about your design thinking approach.

Your opportunity will also be influenced by larger trends and uncertainties in the environment, and secondary research is a great place to quickly explore the broader context of your project. Look for research reports summarizing industry trends, press releases from competitors, or articles in association magazines. Fire up your favorite search engine and explore a bit.

Question 1

What do I already know about my business and customers or users that might matter to my project?

Question 2

What are some of the trends and uncertainties in the larger environment surrounding my project?

	Relevant Trends	Big Uncertainties
Industry		
Target Customer		
Technology		
Society		

Direct Observation

Innovative solutions depend upon fresh insights, and direct observation often yields the crucial clues. As researchers of the user experience, we need to eliminate our own biases and learn more about the discrepancy between what people say and what people do. Through the practice of direct observation, we can uncover unexpected attitudes, behaviors, and embedded meanings that will allow us to generate truly innovative solutions.

At its core, direct observation is about stepping into the user's "native habitat" and capturing the full context, without interpretation or judgment. Imagine you are part of a talented, multidisciplinary team of scientists and that you alone have been selected to go to the field. Your colleagues are waiting for you to return with every clue possible.

Typically the sample size for your direct observation effort will be small—often 8 to 20 subjects in total—but you will make scores of observations about each subject. The goal is not statistical certainty but the cultivation of new hypotheses that can be explored later.

The most important element is to make factual observations devoid of judgment and interpretation. The tips at right will guide your research process and set you up for success.

See D4G page 64 for additional detail and examples.

Tips to Guide Your Research

Set the scene. Record the time, date, and place where you are observing. Are you attending a particular event? Who is present in the environment?

Observe physical space. When you walk into a room or environment, notice how it is set up. What artifacts are in the room? What is the smell? The temperature? Is it dark and stuffy? Or light and breezy? Is the music too loud to hear voices?

Observe the people. Who is present? What is their age? Are they clean-shaven? Is there mud on their shoes? What are they wearing? What colors do they wear? If you know their names, jot them down.

Observe group interactions. Are people standing in groups? What is their attitude towards one another? Is one person always the first to talk?

Observe non-verbal behaviors. Are people laughing? Smiling? What is their body language? Facial expressions? Who is making eye contact? Crossing their arms?

Just the facts. Avoid judgment and interpretation at all costs. An observation is: The two women are facing each other and laughing. An interpretation is: The two women are friends or one woman just said something funny.

Record with your hands and with tools. Our memories are not cameras, and few of us are reliable about little details. That's why using a camera or other recording device can be particularly helpful when you review your written observations later.

Zero in on the unexpected. One way you can organize your notes is to jot down unexpected observations in the margins. Use your intuition—things that jump out at you now might develop into questions and insights later on.

Ethnographic Interviews

Ethnography is the study of human cultures. For innovation and growth teams, this means studying users in ways that capture the full context of their experience, including behaviors, attitudes, beliefs, and cultural meaning. The goal is to identify unmet, unarticulated needs that will help you create a compelling new solution. Here are the steps to follow:

1. **Select people to interview.** You might identify specific individuals based on their relationship to your challenge, or pick random people who share the primary characteristics of your primary stakeholders.

2. **Develop an interview guide.** Keep your questions open-ended and exploratory. Questions that begin with, "Tell me about a time when … " can be particularly useful.

3. **Make contact and schedule your interviews.** Ethnographic interviewing techniques require time to establish rapport and explore topics deeply, so plan on 60 to 120 minutes for each interview.

4. **Conduct your interviews.** Consider making an audio or video recording (with the interviewee's permission). If you can't record the interview, capture as many details and verbatim comments as possible in your notes. Try to interview in pairs.

5. **Be curious about everything.** Encourage the interviewee to elaborate and look for signs of emotion.

6. **Capture your findings.** Review your notes and identify the key takeaways from each interview, creating a one- or two-page summary. Be sure to include actual quotes from the interview that capture the discussion and highlight the interviewee's reality and unmet needs. You'll use these later to share your findings.

TOOLS

Tips for the Interviewing Process

Orient, but don't prime. Tell users the general nature of your interest, and assure their privacy, but don't prime them for what you hope to find.

"I'm researching the way people shop for clothes."

Ask short, factual questions. This is to avoid priming users, and to maximize the productivity of the interview.

"When do you shop? How often? Whom do you go with?"
"Do you have a plan? Do you bring a list?"

Get specific examples. Move quickly past general statements by zeroing in on a specific example.

"Show me something you bought recently.
Tell me how you bought it."

Walk backward, then forward. Interviewees will start with what they see as the action. It is the ethnographer's job to uncover the pre-action and the reaction.

"When did you first decide you needed that?"
"When you see that in your closet now,
what do you think?"

Ask attitudinal questions last. Eventually you will ask users what they think and feel. Careful: If you ask this early, it may color all their responses.

Document artifacts and tools. Actually, document everything; get a picture of what they bought recently.

Record the interview. And be sure to document the tools they use; a list, a smartphone, the websites they look at, the shopping bags they keep, etc.

Listen for attitudes, values, beliefs. There are keywords that signal these emotional states. Be sure to note them when you review the interview later. Absolutes such as "always" and "never" are examples. So are judging phrases such as "deserved" and "should have." Any word or phrase that suggests a perceived lack of choice, or points to an external authority, provides clues to the hidden beliefs people hold.

"In my family, we always ..."
"It just seems like you're expected to ..."
"I always prefer to ..."
"I was stuck having to ..."
"He deserved it ..."
"I should have ..."

Job to Be Done

This tool looks at users' behavior on the basis of their underlying needs, rather than the traditional marketing lens of demographic segmentation. JTBD fundamentally repositions the question from "What do customers want?" to "What job do they want their purchases to do?" A person doesn't want to own a quarter-inch drill, for example, but instead wants to hire a quarter-inch drill to do the job of creating a quarter-inch hole. JTBD is a way to understand what motivates a customer to seek a solution. We are then able to identify gaps in the market and build solutions for specific "jobs."

1. Start by identifying the needs that arise in your stake-holders' lives. Think more broadly than the product you sell or the service you provide or the benefit you deliver. Instead, look for an underlying driver or motivation.

2. Consider the type(s) of jobs to be done. Functional jobs are tasks to be completed and emotional jobs are feelings to achieve or experience. Emotional jobs can be personal jobs (how the stakeholder wants to feel about himself or herself) or social jobs (how the stakeholder wants to be perceived by others).

3. Define the job to be done (the stakeholder's desired outcome) using a simple statement made up of an action verb, an object of action, and a contextual clarifier. Example: A Blackberry helps a business user make efficient use of small snippets of time.

4. List the performance criteria that stakeholders use to make decisions about how to meet the identified need.

5. Describe how the stakeholder currently addresses the identified need. What pain points or dissatisfaction arises as a result?

6. Explore the benchmarks that exist for competing and analogous offerings.

Ultimately, JTBD is a way to reframe. When the Pfizer team members observed that smokers ages 25 to 35 really needed support in making a new lifestyle choice, they were identifying a different job for Nicorette to do. And Nicorette wasn't enough; it needed coaching and social support components. That reframing led them to a new growth platform.

Think about buying a car:

	Stakeholder's Desired Outcome	Metric of Success	Outcomes to Avoid
Functional Job	Providing reliable transportation around town	Always available	Repair costs Breakdowns
Emotional Job	Looking fashionable for my friends	Number of compliments	Snide remarks Other people with the same vehicle

Or shipping a package:

	Stakeholder's Desired Outcome	Metric of Success	Outcomes to Avoid
Functional Job	Delivering goods to another location	Goods received on time and in good condition	Late or lost packages Damaged goods
Emotional Job	Showing the recipient that the contents are important	Acknowledgement of receipt from recipient Positive comments and service rating from recipient	Contents disregarded or overlooked

Or hiring an employee:

	Stakeholder's Desired Outcome	Metric of Success	Outcomes to Avoid
Functional Job	Securing additional resources for the team	Qualified candidate hired Increased team capacity and productivity	Position remains vacant Hired employee is unable to perform to standard
Emotional Job	Looking like a star on the management team	Kudos from boss End-of-year bonus	Accused of brown-nosing Failure to meet targets because of too much time spent on HR issues

Value Chain Analysis

Value chain analysis is the study of your interaction with partners to create value and deliver your offerings to internal or external customers. From it emerge important clues about your partners' capabilities and intentions and your unit's vulnerabilities and opportunities. It is the business-side equivalent of customer journey mapping, highlighting the "pain points" and opportunities in the collaboration with upstream and downstream partners to deliver a product or service.

1. Draw the value chain for your business by identifying each cluster of activities, working backward from the end point of the value delivered to customers. An important (and often tricky) task is defining what constitutes an element in the chain. Remember that we are mapping clusters of activities, not companies.

2. Analyze the competitive environment in each box, identifying the key players.

3. Identify the core strategic capabilities needed to produce the value in each box. What does each contribute to creating value?

4. Evaluate the bargaining power and influence of each player. Who drives performance? How easy would it be to find a substitute? How much value does the end customer perceive is contributed by this player?

5. Determine the possibilities for improving your power and profitability in the chain.

6. Assess your vulnerabilities. Where are you vulnerable to others who might change their footprint in ways that put you at a disadvantage?

7. Identify themes related to bargaining power, capabilities, partners, and defensibility.

See D4G pages 75-80 for additional detail and examples.

Making the business case

What is the potential value capture of different roles in the network?

- Who drives performance?
- Who has customer loyalty?
- Where does the strategic intent align and diverge?

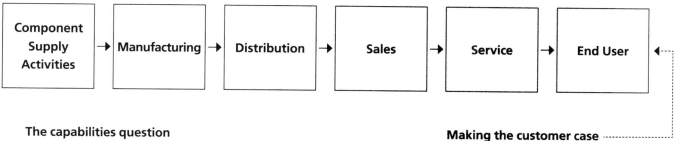

The capabilities question

For each activity cluster in the value chain, what skills and processes are needed to succeed?

The positioning question

Where are we vulnerable?
What possibilities exist to shift/strengthen our role in ways that
  improve our ability to create and capture value?
What new capabilities do we need to develop or improve to do this?
Who should our partners be?

Making the customer case

How does the network create and enhance value as *defined by the customer*?

Journey Mapping

Journey mapping is the representation, in a flowchart or other graphic format, of the stakeholder's experience as he or she works to accomplish something of importance to him or her. These maps can depict the stakeholder's actual or ideal journey. Journey maps can be used throughout the design thinking process and are especially valuable during **What *is*** as a method for documenting stakeholders' current reality.

1. Select the stakeholder whose experience you want to understand more fully. Spend some time investigating his or her context and situation. (An ethnographic interview is a great way to do that. You may also want to observe stakeholders going about their work, watching to see what they actually do as opposed to simply what they say they do.)

2. Decide where the process you want to depict begins and ends. You will want to start a little bit before and extend a little bit after the specific time that your product or service might be used.

3. Using the journey map template on the next page, plot each step of the process you've identified as a point on the journey (you may need to add more steps, but try to keep the total number of steps under a dozen). Above each step, label the person or institution that is primarily responsible for completing the step.

4. Plot the stakeholder's emotional state at each step in the journey in the space indicated. Connect these points with a line.

5. Circle two or three of the emotional high points of the journey. Label each high point with a short description about what made it a high point.

6. Circle two or three of the emotional low points of the journey. Label each low point with a short description about what made it a low point.

7. Imagine your stakeholder's perfect world. If everything went smoothly, what would be the best parts? Using a different color pen or pencil, draw the best-case scenario of the emotions that your stakeholder would experience throughout the journey and connect these points with a line.

8. Reflect on your work. The map you've created reflects multiple dimensions: sequence, responsible party, and emotional variability. Look at the entire map and see what jumps out at you. What patterns do you notice? Which steps have the most opportunity for improvement?

See D4G pages 61-65 for additional detail and examples.

The Journey of

Responsible Party

Description of Step

1	2	3	4	5	6

TOOLS

Emotional High

Neutral

Emotional Low

Notes & References

Personas

Personas are archetypes—fictional characters we create that typify different types of stakeholders. Though we create them based on the real information that we gather during our **What** *is* research, they usually represent a synthesis of characteristics of different people we have interviewed, rather than one actual person. We use them to bring our stakeholders to life—not as demographic descriptions or people to be sold to but as flesh-and-blood people with names, challenges, hopes, and dreams. We then use these to try to identify particular design criteria and design specific new solutions for each attractive persona.

You can develop your own personas in three steps:

1. Study the themes you have uncovered in your research to identify a number of dimensions, usually psychographic rather than demographic, that you believe help reveal the differences within the group of stakeholders you learned about. (We find a list of universal human needs, compiled by the Center for Nonviolent Communication, to be very useful in generating dimensions and have included it on page 104.)

2. Select a number of dimensions that you feel are revealing. Experiment by pairing two different sets of dimensions to create a 2x2 matrix, and then map

each actual interviewee into whatever quadrant seems to fit best. Continue to try new variations until you find a pair of dimensions that seems to distribute your interviewees across at least three of the four quadrants.

For example, "social behavior" might be one dimension, with "introverted" at one extreme and "extroverted" at the other. You might cross it with "spending habits" and use "frugal" and "free-spending" as the extremes.

3. Create a persona who belongs in each quadrant. Describe the archetype as fully as possible, focusing on the demographics and psychographics that make this archetype unique.

You may want to combine your results with the journey mapping approach. Map the journey of each persona. Each should reveal its own set of low points. These are the "pain points" that represent the most valuable innovation opportunities for that customer type. While some low points may be shared across personas (making them a particularly fruitful target for innovation), we want to generate some new ideas designed specifically for the persona in each quadrant.

See D4G pages 67-71 for additional detail and examples.

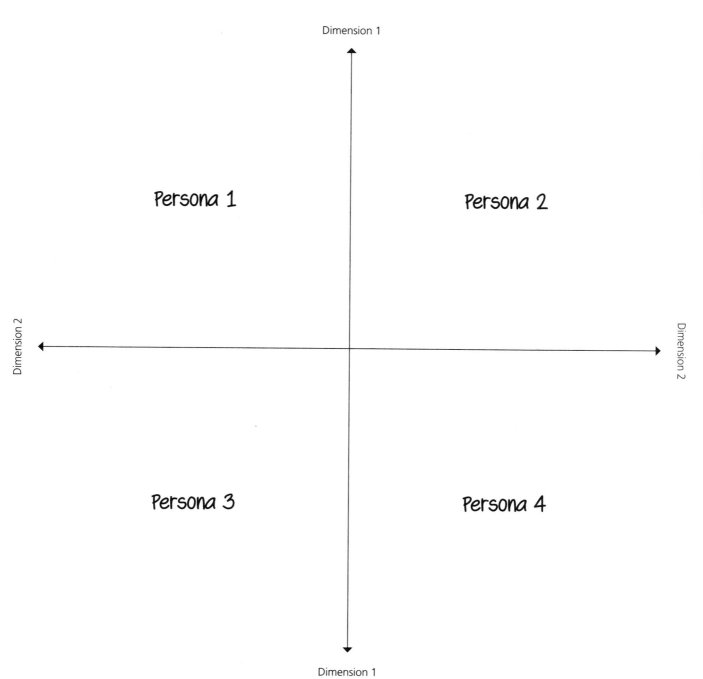

360 Empathy

Brainstorming can easily generate a hundred ideas for a particular challenge. But which few of the hundred are worth exploring further? The ones that are most responsive to the unmet needs. The sensing of unmet needs—especially unarticulated needs—requires deep empathy with users. One of the simplest methods to forge this emotional connection is through 360 empathy. You can use this analytic approach immediately after conducting ethnographic interviews or direct observation.

Using the template, we can connect with the user's emotional world by entering through his or her senses. Start by labeling the challenge or opportunity using 20 words or less. Then move through the template in numerical order, from step 1 to step 6. The sequence helps you work from the outside in, starting with the information entering through the user's eyes and ears, then what he or she is doing and saying, and finally into the emotional realm of feelings and needs. Only for these final two categories—feelings and needs—do we apply judgment and conjecture. The information that is entered here is not factual. Furthermore, it is often inherently contradictory; that is, one entry *might* directly contradict the entry noted just above it. The purpose is to identify what is true for the user, in an effort to isolate a latent need that has not been articulated directly.

To help distinguish feelings from needs, we recommend using the list of universal human feelings and universal human needs that was published by the Center for Non-violent Communication. The full lists are provided in the Resources section, pages 99-105.

AREA OF OPPORTUNITY

Describe the challenge/opportunity. Keep this short (20 words or less). Use the design brief for reference.

1. SEEING

Note the information that enters through the user's eyes. What is he or she literally seeing in relation to the challenge?

2. HEARING

What experiences occur to the user as sounds? In addition to words he or she hears, include ambient sounds that are integral to the experience.

3. DOING

Note the key physical movements and behaviors that accompany the challenge. The data from direct observation will be the most insightful here.

4. SAYING

Summarize the most revealing verbatim words and phrases he or she uses when speaking about the challenge.

5. FEELING? (GUESSES)

Make guesses about what you believe the user may be feeling. Don't worry if your guesses contradict each other; look for breadth of possibilities to explore.

Note: See the CNVC List of Universal Human Feelings on page 100.

6. LATENT NEED? (GUESSES)

Create a short list of possible unmet needs that may exist for the user. Use the results of Step 5 to spur the discussion. The goal is not consensus among the team but a sense that there are intriguing possibilities to fuel the brainstorming sessions that will follow. The insights here will be essential to create a strong reframe.

Note: See the CNVC List of Universal Human Needs on page 104.

TOOLS

Creating Posters

Once you've gathered this much data, the next challenge is to figure out how to share it. In a lot of our organizations, we find that this quickly becomes an exercise in PowerPoint. We put oodles of information into charts and graphs and tables and bullet points. Then, we either ask people to read it on their own or we bring everyone into a conference room and walk through it slide by slide.

We prefer a different approach when it comes to sharing our findings in **What *is*.** We like to use posters: sheets of paper, roughly 24 x 36 inches or larger, that depict elements of the data that you've collected. Posters create a visual focal point for the conversations that will follow. Because everyone on your team can view a poster at once, it creates a shared perspective on the data. And because it doesn't disappear with the click of a button, you and your team can refer to it throughout your work.

Here's how to create your posters:

1. Review the data you've collected and make a list of the information you want to share. You might include some of your individual interviews, or results of your secondary research, or some of what you've generated from the other **What *is*** tools.

2. Refine your list to about 25 to 30 posters. Although it can be hard to limit yourself, more isn't necessarily better. Think about curating your list of posters the way a museum curator might put together an exhibit, and select the poster topics that will help create interesting conversations about your project.

3. Prepare your data. You'll want your posters to be as close to the source of your data as possible. That means that for posters showcasing your ethnographic interviews, you should use direct quotations from your interview subjects. For posters of quantitative data, display the information without added interpretation. Be careful not to let your own assumptions or conclusions obstruct the data itself, since the goal will be to invite everyone on the team to help find insights.

4. Produce the posters. You can create them in word processing or presentation software, and then have them enlarged and printed at your local copy shop. (In most areas, we're able to get a black-and-white poster print made for about $5.) Don't have access to a print shop? You can also create your posters by writing your information on flip-chart pages. Just make sure you write neatly.

Sample Ethnographic Interview Summary Poster

First name:

Age:

Occupation:

Relationship to challenge:

Descriptive information (e.g., favorite magazines, typical attire, typical day):

Quotes from your interview that showcase the person's attitude, behavior, and needs relative to your challenge:

TOOLS

Brainstorming

We think it's a good idea to use two or three different brainstorming techniques, so choose a couple from among the following.

#1 Blue Cards and Trigger Questions

Traditional blue-sky brainstorming can generate new ideas, but these sessions are often bogged down by extroverts and rehashed ideas from last year. Instead of blue sky, try a session using blue *cards.* Here's how you do it:

1. Develop a list of trigger questions that range from the familiar ("How will mobile affect this problem?") to the provocative ("How could crowdsourcing be used here?"). The more customized to your challenge, the better.

2. Present the first trigger question to the group, and invite each person to work silently and write down at least three ideas on blue cards (or Post-it notes), one idea per card. Allow about three minutes for a round of writing.

3. Ask each person to read their cards and pin them on a board (one at a time, without long explanations). Don't worry about sorting the cards at this point.

4. When all the cards are posted, have a second round with the same trigger question. This gives people a chance to build on the round 1 ideas and to dig deeper. Round 2 ideas are often the most intriguing.

5. Repeat the process with the second trigger question, and so forth. Five or six trigger questions easily can generate eighty-plus unique ideas in a five-person group.

The blue-card method does a great job of making sure the savvy introvert gets a voice in the brainstorm process. It also offsets the "boss effect," where people wait for the senior person to show his or her cards before chiming in. Most importantly, it has been proven to generate three times as many ideas as facilitated oral brainstorming, even after eliminating redundancies.

TOOLS

5 Pre-written Trigger Questions

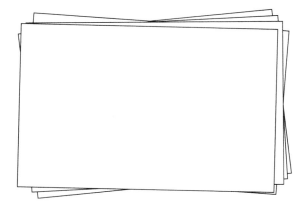

5 Brainstormers

100 Blue Cards

40 Minutes

#2 Analogies/Thief and Doctor

Analogies are a natural way to see new possibilities. Analogies answer the question, "Where else do these conditions occur, and what has been done to solve them?" A simple way to stimulate analogies is to convert the user's circumstances into a list of attributes and then brainstorm other situations that share some of those attributes. You'll become a "thief" as you steal elements of the analogous solutions, and then you'll "doctor" them to fit your context.

For example, when Christi Zuber at Kaiser Permanente wanted to find an innovative solution for nurse medication rounds, she and her team looked for analogies. One attribute they noted was that nurses need 100% concentration on their task during medication rounds but are required to multitask at other times.

The role of airplane pilots struck them as an analogy. Takeoff and landing are crucial moments, but the pilot's role during the rest of the flight is often less demanding. When they visited an airline crew, Christi and her team learned about "the sterile cockpit," which is a time period when no one is allowed to speak except the pilot and co-pilot, and they can speak only about takeoff or landing.

The template on this page can be used to facilitate a brainstorming session to identify analogies. In the "User Context" box you might write "Nurse medication rounds," for example. Then list the top five or six attributes that describe the context. These might include "high-risk environment, time pressure, many potential distractions, temporary role change," and so forth.

Next, start brainstorming with the key attributes as your trigger questions. Place your Post-it notes on the bull's-eye, ranging from "mild" (highly similar context) to "wild" (very dissimilar analogies that stretch our thinking).

Finally, it is time to *adapt* the analogies to your context. What opportunities do you see to translate a business practice from the analogy to your context? (Better yet, think about making a site visit to that business, as Christi Zuber and her team did.)

See D4G pages 103-110 for additional detail and examples.

User Context

Key Attributes

Analogies

WILD

MILD

Adaptation

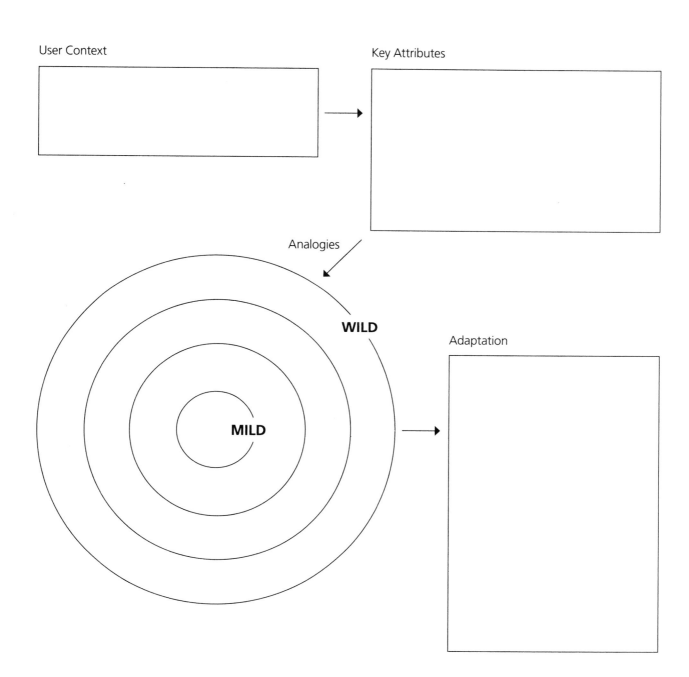

More Brainstorming Techniques

Of course, there are dozens more ways to brainstorm. Here we list three methods that we've found successful. Feel free to try variants of them, as well.

Worst Idea

Fear of looking ill-informed, out-of-touch, or just plain silly often inhibits brainstorming and keeps ideas "safe." By focusing on intentionally bad ideas first, we can reduce that barrier and spark breakthrough thinking.

1. State your objective for the group and familiarize everyone with your design criteria.

2. Working as a group, make a list of 20 (or more) intentionally bad ideas. The worse, the better.

   These could include:

   - Ideas that would achieve the opposite of your objective
   - Ideas that are so extreme or over-the-top that they would be impractical
   - Ideas based on resources that don't exist or technology that hasn't yet been developed
   - Ideas that go against convention or have a significant flaw in logic

3. Using your bad ideas as inspiration, try to "flip" each one into a relatively good idea. If possible, create one or more genuine ideas from each bad idea.

4. Stretch yourself. Are any of your bad ideas actually good?

Contra-Logic

One of our favorite ways to trigger new insights is to invite brainstorm participants to act as contrarians. There's a catch: Instead of asking them to contradict everything, we focus their attention on the underlying elements that make the current business work. We call these the "dominant logic" of the business.

1. Create a list of the underlying assumptions that typically define your industry, function, or service.

2. For each assumption, develop an alternate reality or perspective. Often you can do this by replacing a word with its opposite or inserting the word "not" into the statement.

3. Imagine that this alternate reality is true, and generate ideas that might achieve your objective given these conditions.

For example, imagine you are a recent graduate of the Cordon Bleu and you're looking for an innovative way to provide high-end gastronomical experiences. You might identify an underlying assumption that you need a high-end retail location, flip it to imagine that you can serve your delicious food anywhere, and generate an idea for a gourmet food truck.

Change Perspectives

Diversity of thought can be an invaluable resource when generating ideas, but often our teams share similar expertise and experience. This technique can help you adopt the experience (or inexperience) of virtual team members without the hassles of scheduling, time travel, or damage to your travel and entertainment (T&E) budget.

1. State your objective and design criteria.

2. Select at least five different perspectives to help you generate ideas. Possible perspectives include:

    - Middle school teacher
    - Bill Gates
    - Superhero
    - Your primary competitor
    - Oprah
    - Used car salesman

3. Consider how each of your chosen perspectives might approach or address your problem. Try to generate at least ten possibilities from each of your selected perspectives.

4. How can you adapt these perspectives to help solve your problem?

Anchors

After brainstorming is when many innovation teams get stuck, and it's easy to see why. Either they can't decide what to do next, or they decide to do one—and only one—thing. Both are failure modes. And in both cases, choosing good concept anchors is the way out.

Consider the innovation team that brainstorms 100 ideas, struggles to form them into three to five concepts, and then observes that there really are just a few elements they all believe in. So they decide in the conference room which single concept to take forward. This last step is a mistake! Many of our high-potential concepts never see the light of day, ending up instead in a trash can in the conference room. Design thinking is user-driven, and that includes empowering users to consider multiple concepts and shape what emerges.

Strong alternatives come from choosing anchors to form distinctive concepts, each of which will be shown to customers as a visual prototype. Anchors keep us from stacking the deck for a single all-encompassing solution; they ensure that we provide genuine choices to customers in co-creation.

Well-chosen anchors provide the gravitational pull to bring various elements of a concept into a coherent whole.

Tips for Choosing Anchors

Themes – Unique vs. Shared. After brainstorming potential solution elements, have the group identify eight to ten themes that emerged. Example themes might be: analytics, social media, self-service, concierge service, mobile, risk-sharing. Choose three or four of the themes to be unique, used in only one concept. Self-service, risk-sharing, and concierge could be distinct anchors, for example. The other elements and themes may be used multiple times. This will result in three distinct alternative concepts to prototype and share with target customers.

Vary the Focal Point. Choose two or three different types of users as the focal point for distinct concepts. For a health care concept, for example, you might choose chronic disease patients.

End-to-End vs. Targeted. Many solutions have the option to be end-to-end experiences or to go deep on a key aspect. You can use these distinctions as anchors to see what customers value most.

Mechanics vs. Humanics. It is easy to just throw technology at a given challenge, but a more human-driven approach is sometimes possible, too. If so, use human-driven as one of the anchors, and see what emerges.

Business Models. Most new products and services also present new business model opportunities. Choose a nontraditional business model—such as subscription-based or risk-sharing—as an anchor.

Bring-Build-Buy Map

Forming concepts requires us to link the demand chain—based on our user insights—with a supply chain capable of meeting that demand. To see new possibilities in the supply chain, it can be helpful to draw a map of the relevant capabilities and which firms might provide them.

The Bring-Build-Buy map shown here is a way to see those possibilities. Think of it as a make-buy template with unmet needs as the North Star.

Set the template up on a poster or whiteboard, with room for eight to ten Post-it notes in each of the rectangles.

Complete this template in the order of Bring, then Build, and finally Buy. There will be multiple Bring-Build-Buy solutions possible, of course, each with different strategic strengths and weaknesses.

For example, if you are Pfizer and wish to provide a smoking cessation service, the elements you might *bring* could include Nicorette and global distribution. You might *build* an e-commerce transaction capability. You might *buy* phone-based counseling services (that is, get that capability through a partner).

These choices affect both the concept and the potential business model. This tool helps you see the possibilities. It can set the stage for forced connections and/or combinatorial play (the next two tools).

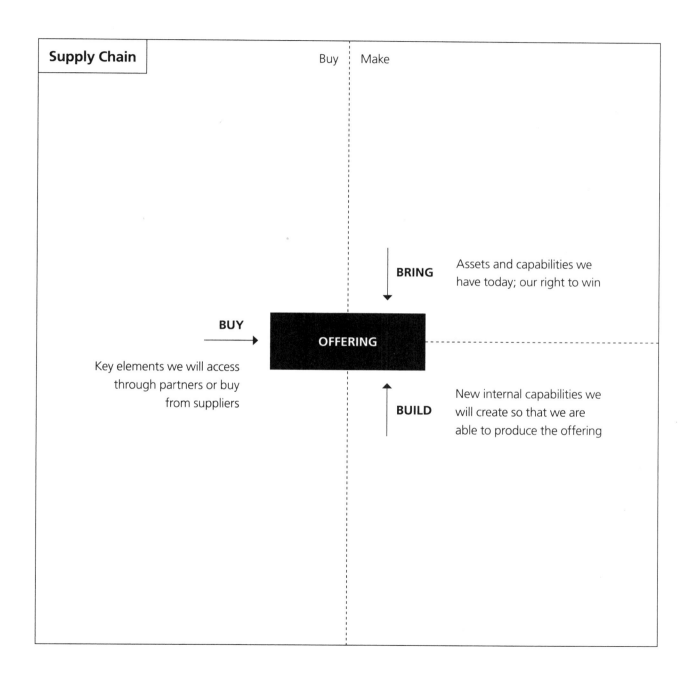

Supply Chain

Buy | Make

BRING — Assets and capabilities we have today; our right to win

BUY — Key elements we will access through partners or buy from suppliers

OFFERING

BUILD — New internal capabilities we will create so that we are able to produce the offering

Forced Connections

TOOLS

Serendipity and surprise are powerful drivers of creativity in the concept development process. The forced connections method of building concepts stretches our minds to find links in unexpected places by juxtaposing seemingly unrelated outputs of your brainstorming as the building blocks of new concepts.

This method is best used with a group of four to six people. Begin with the Post-it notes you generated during your brainstorming.

1. Look at all the ideas you have posted. Individually, take a minute to consider which ideas or combination of ideas you think deserve further focus.

2. Get three people from your group to each silently (and independently) select one idea.

3. Place the three ideas together and force connections to generate three or more interesting, novel, or "impossible" concepts.

4. Repeat steps 2 and 3 at least four times (more is better; try to keep at it for 45 minutes or so).

5. Transfer the most promising concepts/ideas to large notes and proceed to the next step (Create Some Napkin Pitches).

Select some of the most intriguing ideas and see if you can force them together here.

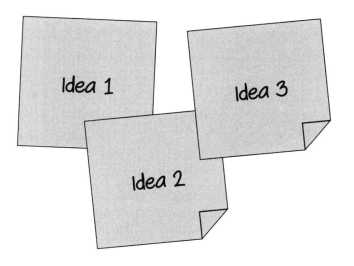

Forced Connection
Concept 1

Forced Connection
Concept 2

Forced Connection
Concept 3

Combinatorial Play

Combinatorial play is a systematic way of mixing and matching the "ingredients" of your ideas. Remember back in algebra class when you learned about combinations and permutations? Suffice it to say that when you start to play mix-and-match, a handful of individual ideas can transform into a mountain of possible concepts. Some of the resulting combinations might be wacky (or downright nonsensical), but this method of concept development will ensure that you don't overlook any possible solutions.

1. Gather your brainstormed ideas.

2. Clean up your list of ideas by eliminating redundancies, seeing what is missing, and adding ideas where possible.

3. Group similar ideas next to each other. Think about different kinds of groupings, like the different categories of ingredients you can use when making chili.

4. Form initial concepts (build your chili recipes). This step combines different elements from the brainstorming to form distinctive concepts. One of our favorite approaches is to set up a "chili table." Here's how it goes:

    - Across the top, list the categories of ideas you used for your groupings. These are your "ingredient categories"—in this case, things you can put into chili, like meat, beans, veggies, spices, etc.

    - Now list the ideas from each grouping into their respective columns in your table.

    - Now create different combinations of the individual ideas to make different kinds of chili. You might make vegetarian chili (lots of veggies, no meat), meat lover's chili (every kind of meat, no veggies), or Hawaiian chili (ham and pineapple, hold the cayenne pepper). You get the idea.

    - Once you've exhausted the obvious combinations, have some fun playing with "crazy" combinations. See what happens if you randomly select an idea from each ingredient category. What new chili variations can you concoct?

See D4G pages 114-117 for additional detail and examples.

Chili Table

CATEGORIES

IDEAS

Visualization Basics

Visualization is fundamental to design thinking, and it has application at every step of the process. Remember, we are envisioning an improved future, working in the unknown, and relying on collaborators to help shape the results. So we depend upon visual methods to make our thinking accessible to others, so they can contribute to the problem-solving process.

Different forms of visualization are appropriate at different stages. Step 12, Make Prototypes, describes several forms that may be useful at that step. The full range of choices includes:

- Storytelling (described more on page 78)
- Role-playing
- Poster
- Photo montage
- Flowchart
- Storyboarding (described more on page 80)
- Video
- Business concept illustration (yes, even Power-Point might qualify as visualization)

Note that not all of these forms of visualization actually involve drawing. Even for those methods that are visual in a traditional sense, artistic skills are not required.

To get started, pick your visualization tools:

- Field notebook – to serve as a constant reference
- Pencil – unless you never erase, then a pen is fine
- Digital camera – indispensible tool
- Whiteboard – best if it is on wheels
- Dry erase markers – in multiple colors
- Post-it notes – various sizes and colors
- Sharpies – the best friend a Post-it ever had
- Flip-chart paper – and longer rolls of butcher paper, for that matter
- Wall space – this is crucial as a way to share current ideas
- Windows – write on them with dry erase markers or use them as a vertical work space

See D4G pages 49-60 for additional detail and examples.

Principles for Creating Visuals

Just do it. Give up any notion of whether you are good at drawing. Just start scribbling.

Fewest words wins. Convey the ideas using the fewest words and labels.

Incomplete. Skip the details and leave it a bit incomplete, so others can bring their insights to the process.

People first. Put people at the center of your visualization. The time for wiring diagrams will come later.

Rough and ready. It should look like you cranked it out in a few minutes.

Guidelines for Using Visuals

Share at "good enough." Don't waste time on artistry. Put it out there.

Leave them on display. Visual communications need to go on a wall where others can see them. That's the whole point.

Invite co-authorship. Have Post-its and Sharpies handy. The moment someone draws over it—voila—you've enabled co-creation!

Fossil record. When the visual is outdated, don't throw it away. Just put the new one over it. The walls of the project room will become the fossil record of the project.

Your visuals can and should be basic. The elements below may be all you need to create simple sketches that give shape and context to your ideas. Give it a try.

Rectangle	Setting	Stick Figure	Tools	Speech	Thought
	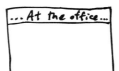				

Storytelling

Stories are an innovator's best friend. They bring collaborators to a project the way nectar brings bees to a flower. That's because stories are a time-efficient, memorable way to answer both the "What" and the "So What?" of a project. The human brain receives facts and data, but it participates in stories by:

- Visualizing the details
- Rooting for the protagonist
- Investing in the outcome

These elements are crucial to help your collaborators suspend their skepticism and help you discover what might be possible. The story can take many forms, including (1) a short prose narrative, (2) a series of images you speak to, (3) a storyboard, or even (4) a video. All of the forms rely on imagery to invite the listener's participation.

Elements to Bring Collaborators on Board

Hero. A customer the listener will care about

Supporting characters.
Antagonist: Forces that work against the hero; Unexpected ally: Your solution

Setting. The context where the action takes place

Plot exposition. The movement of the protagonist toward his or her goal

Tension. A conflict between the protagonist's goal and reality; also called the "rising action"

Climax. A moment of transformation when your solution opens up an unexpected path to the goal

Resolution. What we make of things after the dust settles

To build a story of your growth project, create a narrative that roughly follows this outline:

Meet …	*hero / user*
She is a …	*role*
with a penchant for …	*personal attribute*
who wants to …	*goal*
One day she is at …	*setting*
and she tries to …	*move toward goal*
Instead of …	*intended outcome*
she discovers …	*obstacle*
Now she must …	*complication*
Just when she feels …	*authentic emotion*
she is surprised to discover …	*unexpected ally – your solution*
Suddenly …	*path to goal*
Today she is able to …	*simple path to goal*
and she can realize …	*higher-level goal or need*

As a reminder, good stories are **brief** (not more than one or two pages), focused on the **hero,** and rich with **imagery.** Good stories are not value propositions, personas, or elevator pitches.

Storyboarding

A visual story (also referred to as a storyboard) can make your concept even more tangible. Storyboards are useful prototypes any time a concept will change a significant part of the stakeholder's journey. They're particularly handy for things that aren't tangible—like processes or systems—and often serve as a launching pad for co-creation. (Just show your stakeholder a storyboard, and have him or her add key dialog or narration.)

The storyboard itself looks a bit like a cartoon strip from the Sunday funnies. It's a series of six to ten glimpses into the stakeholder's journey or the concept in action. Building a storyboard from scratch doesn't require great drawing skill. It only takes the courage to create a few sketches. (If you want to give it a try but don't know where to start, pick up a copy of *The Back of the Napkin* by Dan Roam for some tips.)

Sometimes, though, even the simplest of drawings can seem a bit paralyzing. If that's the case, you'll find some core storyboard elements in the Templates section to get you started. Make photocopies of the drawings and cut them out to get your storyboard started, and embellish each panel with the details that bring your concept to life. Fill in the details with your own sketches. And remember, sometimes a rough sketch results in the most useful feedback, so don't work too hard to make your illustrations perfect.

See D4G pages 55-58 for additional detail and examples.

TOOLS

Co-Creation Tools

Any time a potential user helps you modify or enhance your concept, that represents co-creation. Co-creation always relies on stimulus—some representation of a concept that the user can interact with, whether physically or with his or her imagination. Here are some of the most useful co-creation tools we've found.

Storyboard – linear, narrated

The storyboard is a great format because it so efficiently communicates the experience while leaving plenty of white space for users to overlay their interpretation. A linear storyboard takes them on a fixed route, like a train. If you use a linear storyboard, be sure to present an alternative storyboard alongside it, with a different route, so users can consider different ways to solve their problem. This side-by-side approach invites mixing and matching, as in, "I wish storyboard A could include the second panel from storyboard B." Bingo—that's what you need to know. Users may interact with the storyboard by placing green dots on the appealing aspects and red dots on the annoying parts. Or they can place Post-it notes on the panels with comments and questions. Having them physically interact with the storyboard is crucial, since it shifts their mind-set from "validation" to "participation." Having users stand up and work on a poster is better than a seated co-creation session, because their body language is more pronounced when they are standing.

Storyboard – build-your-own, configurable

A less prescriptive version of the storyboard is to show features on individual panels and let users configure the experience themselves. Spread out the panels on a table and let them "shop" for the features that are appealing to them. Be sure to have some blank panels so they can invent the experience elements they want but don't see in the stack. Other interactions match the linear storyboard.

Cartoon – with blank speech bubbles

A great way to let users express their emotional needs is to populate a storyboard or story panels with characters that have blank speech (or thought) bubbles above them. This way they can write the dialog and build their own narrative. Often the most subdued customers will surprise you with their expressiveness in this format.

Card sort

Card sorting lets users consider up to two dozen features or elements and make judgments about their relative value. Prepare by printing the name of the features on index cards (e.g., "live phone coach 24/7"). Ask the respondents to sort the features as either Must-Have, Nice-to-Have, or Indifferent/Omit. Other choice frames are possible, too. Again, much of the value is in what is said about the features and the choices being made.

3D mock-up

For many solutions, it is possible to mock-up the experience in 3D and have users act out their role. For a new hospitality experience in the lobby, for example, build a mock-up at a single property and let people try it out. Users are surprisingly adept at make-believe.

Video prototype

You can make a short video of a person using a new service, then show it to target customers. Ask them to comment on the parts that are appealing to them and the parts that seem unrealistic or unwanted. Give them control of the pause button and record their comments.

Bear in mind that co-creation is your opportunity to let users show you what is most important to them. It is not yet time to show them how well you listened, and it is certainly not the place to "sell" your early prototypes.

Templates

You've reached the end of your field book, but it's not the end of your design thinking journey. We hope that you find many occasions to retrace your steps and apply the design thinking tools and mind-set to the vast array of wicked problems that you face at work and in life.

In this section of your field book, you'll find templates to support each step and tool you've encountered so far. You can use the templates directly in this book, make photocopies, or download digital templates from the Design@Darden website to enlarge to poster size. (We suggest that last option, since posters naturally facilitate the collaboration that design thinking demands.)

Along the way, you might also refer to *Designing for Growth: A Design Thinking Tool Kit for Managers* for more information and inspiration.

From here on out, it's up to you. Have fun!

TEMPLATES

Scoping Template

What is a broader area of opportunity around this?

What is a broader area of opportunity around this?

Ask yourself
What's one reason this matters?

START HERE
Current area of opportunity:

Ask yourself
What's another reason this matters?

Ask yourself
What's one barrier that gets in the way?

Ask yourself
What's another barrier that gets in the way?

What is a narrower area of opportunity focused on this?

What is a narrower area of opportunity focused on this?

TEMPLATES

Design Brief

Project Description	
Scope	
Constraints	
Target Users	
Exploration Questions	
Expected Outcomes	
Success Metrics	

Research Plan

Who or what will we study?	Where will we find the people or information?	What questions/issues will we explore?	Number of observations, interviews, or inputs	When will the research happen?	Who on the team is responsible?

TEMPLATES

The Journey of

Responsible Party

Description of Step

1	2	3	4	5	6

Emotional High

Neutral

Emotional Low

Notes & References

Persona Map

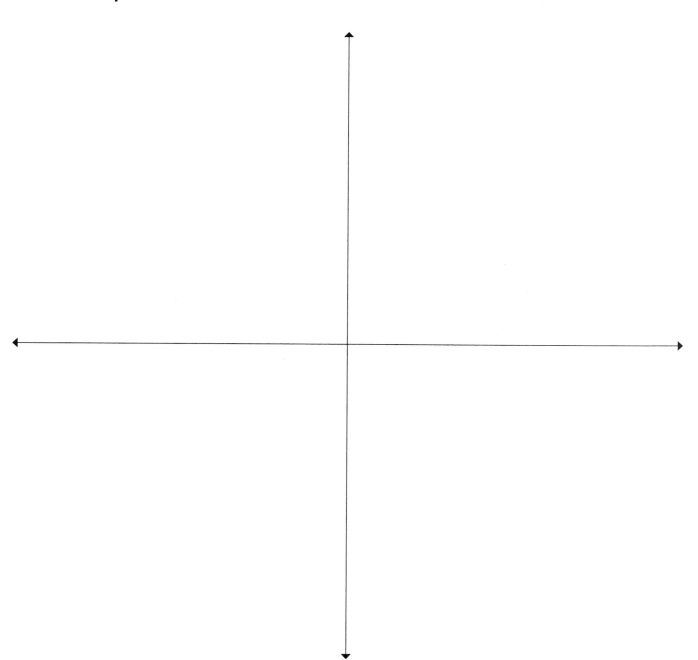

360 Empathy

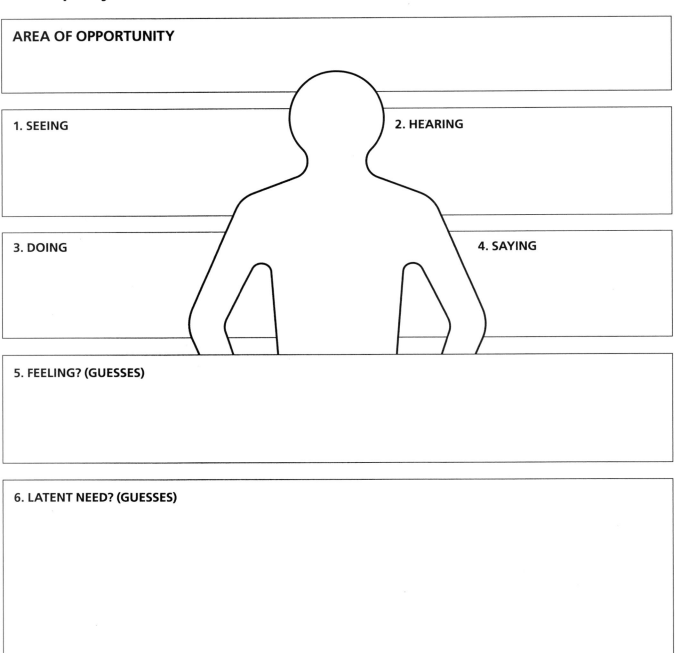

AREA OF OPPORTUNITY

1. SEEING

2. HEARING

3. DOING

4. SAYING

5. FEELING? (GUESSES)

6. LATENT NEED? (GUESSES)

Chili Table

CATEGORIES

IDEAS

Napkin Pitch

CONCEPT NAME:

The Big Idea	Needs/Benefits

Execution	Business Rationale

Storyboards

Sample Storyboard "Scenes"

Learning Launch Design

Key Assumptions to Test	Learning Launch # _____
	Who
	Where
	How
	Cost
	Time
Key Assumptions to Test	**Learning Launch # _____**
	Who
	Where
	How
	Cost
	Time

What to Watch For

Untested Assumptions	Success Metric	Disconfirming Data

Resources

List of Universal Human Feelings

Here is a list of universal human feelings, provided by the Center for Nonviolent Communication (CNVC). The CNVC is a nonprofit organization dedicated to furthering the principles of nonviolence. CNVC believes that we all share the same basic human feelings and needs.

Feelings are different from needs, of course, since they reflect our emotional state. Design researchers can use feelings as a window through which to see unmet needs. The 360 Empathy tool has a section for feelings, but feelings are relevant to every part of the design thinking process that relies on empathy.

Feelings when your needs are satisfied:

AFFECTIONATE

Compassionate
Friendly
Loving
Open hearted
Sympathetic
Tender
Warm

ENGAGED

Absorbed
Alert
Curious
Engrossed
Enchanted
Entranced
Fascinated
Interested
Intrigued
Involved
Spellbound
Stimulated

HOPEFUL

Expectant
Encouraged
Optimistic

CONFIDENT

Empowered
Open
Proud
Safe
Secure

EXCITED

Amazed
Animated
Ardent
Aroused
Astonished
Dazzled
Eager
Energetic
Enthusiastic
Giddy
Invigorated
Lively
Passionate
Surprised
Vibrant

GRATEFUL

Appreciative
Moved
Thankful
Touched

INSPIRED

Amazed
Awed
Wonder

JOYFUL

Amused
Delighted
Glad
Happy
Jubilant
Pleased
Tickled

EXHILARATED

Blissful
Ecstatic
Elated
Enthralled
Exuberant
Radiant
Rapturous
Thrilled

PEACEFUL

Calm
Clear headed
Comfortable
Centered
Content
Equanimous
Fulfilled
Mellow
Quiet
Relaxed
Relieved
Satisfied
Serene
Still
Tranquil
Trusting

REFRESHED

Enlivened
Rejuvenated
Renewed
Rested
Restored
Revived

Feelings when your needs are NOT satisfied:

AFRAID

Apprehensive
Dread
Foreboding
Frightened
Mistrustful
Panicked
Petrified
Scared
Suspicious
Terrified
Wary
Worried

ANNOYED

Aggravated
Dismayed
Disgruntled
Displeased
Exasperated
Frustrated
Impatient
Irritated
Irked

ANGRY

Enraged
Furious
Incensed
Indignant
Irate
Livid
Outraged
Resentful

AVERSION

Animosity
Appalled
Contempt
Disgusted
Dislike
Hate
Horrified
Hostile
Repulsed

CONFUSED

Ambivalent
Baffled
Bewildered
Dazed
Hesitant
Lost
Mystified
Perplexed
Puzzled
Torn

DISCONNECTED

Alienated
Aloof
Apathetic
Bored
Cold
Detached
Distant
Distracted
Indifferent
Numb
Removed
Uninterested
Withdrawn

DISQUIET

Agitated
Alarmed
Discombobulated
Disconcerted
Disturbed
Perturbed
Rattled
Restless
Shocked
Startled
Surprised
Troubled
Turbulent
Turmoil
Uncomfortable
Uneasy
Unnerved
Unsettled
Upset

EMBARRASSED

Ashamed
Chagrined
Flustered
Guilty
Mortified
Self-conscious

RESOURCES

FATIGUE

Beat
Burnt out
Depleted
Exhausted
Lethargic
Listless
Sleepy
Tired
Weary
Worn out

PAIN

Agony
Anguished
Bereaved
Devastated
Grief
Heartbroken
Hurt
Lonely
Miserable
Regretful
Remorseful

SAD

Depressed
Dejected
Despair
Despondent
Disappointed
Discouraged
Disheartened
Forlorn
Gloomy
Heavy hearted
Hopeless
Melancholy
Unhappy
Wretched

TENSE

Anxious
Cranky
Distressed
Distraught
Edgy
Fidgety
Frazzled
Irritable
Jittery
Nervous
Overwhelmed
Restless
Stressed out

VULNERABLE

Fragile
Guarded
Helpless
Insecure
Leery
Reserved
Sensitive
Shaky

YEARNING

Envious
Jealous
Longing
Nostalgic
Pining
Wistful

List of Universal Human Needs

Here is a list of universal human needs, provided by the Center for Nonviolent Communication (CNVC). CNVC believes that we all share the same basic human needs and that each of our actions helps us meet one or more of those needs. Since design thinking is based on the identification of unmet needs, this list can be a valuable tool. It is especially helpful for completing design templates such as 360 Empathy.

CONNECTION

Acceptance
Affection
Appreciation
Belonging
Cooperation
Communication
Closeness
Community
Companionship
Compassion
Consideration
Consistency
Empathy
Inclusion
Intimacy
Love
Mutuality
Nurturing
Respect/self-respect
Safety
Security
Stability
Support
To know and be known
To see and be seen
To understand and be understood
Trust
Warmth

PHYSICAL WELL-BEING

Air
Food
Movement/exercise
Rest/sleep
Sexual expression
Safety
Shelter
Touch
Water

HONESTY

Authenticity
Integrity
Presence

PLAY

Joy
Humor

PEACE

Beauty
Communion
Ease
Equality
Harmony
Inspiration
Order

AUTONOMY

Choice
Freedom
Independence
Space
Spontaneity

MEANING

Awareness
Celebration of life
Challenge
Clarity
Competence
Consciousness
Contribution
Creativity
Discovery
Efficacy
Effectiveness
Growth
Hope
Learning
Mourning
Participation
Purpose
Self-expression
Stimulation
To matter
Understanding

An Example
Project

Setting the Scene

Picture a leading global industrial company (we'll call it Metals R Us, or MRU for short) with annual revenues of $2.5 billion and more than 10,000 employees. In the past decade, MRU received consistent recognition for outstanding financial performance and world-class safety, and was named among *Fortune* magazine's 100 Best Companies to Work For.

A key contributor to MRU's continuing success was its corporate commitment to employee health and well-being. MRU launched an official wellness program in the 1980s with an onsite employee gym in its headquarters. Its programs expanded to include an onsite medical center and pharmacy, multiple health care plan options, a full-time dietician, and trainers. MRU also provides an an optional wellness program managed by an outside vendor, and about half of its workers participate in the program.

Company executives believe that MRU's focus on wellness delivers significant cost savings (reduced health care premiums, higher employee productivity due to reduced absenteeism) and is a tangible demonstration of its corporate values. In recent years, spending on MRU's wellness efforts has yielded an ROI of 2:1 and has signficantly reduced conditions including heart disease, high blood pressure, and diabetes among program participants.

With the rising costs of health care, MRU leaders are increasingly committed to exploring new opportunities to realize the benefits of a healthy workforce. Citing studies that a key driver of successful programs is employee participation, they are particularly interested in developing additional wellness initiatives and policies that engage those employees who aren't currently participating.

Question	Design thinking is appropriate if …	Linear analytic methods may be better if …
Is the problem human-centered?	…ding of the actual …olved is both possible	There are few human beings involved in the problem or the solution
How clearly do you understand the problem itself?	We have a hunch about the p… and/or opportunity, but we n… explore and get agreement	…erstand the problem clearly and …we're solving the right one
What's the level of uncertainty?	There are many unknowns (large and small), and past data is unlikely to help us	The past is a good predictor of the future
What's the degree of complexity?	…many connecting and …ndent facets of the problem; …to know where to start	The path to solving the problem is clear, and analytic methods have succeeded in solving similar problems in the past
What data is already available to …	…s very little relevant existin… to analyze	…everal clear sources of …ata
What's your level of curiosity and influence?	…o explore more and can get …eople willing to help me	The problem feels routine to me, and I have to follow existing processes and systems

Yes. Understanding employee needs related to health is central to the challenge.

Our ultimate objective is clear, but we don't know for sure what barriers we need to address.

Many interconnected elements: insurance, legal constraints, employee morale, financial performance, other initiatives.

We have our historical data and some best practices research, but we don't know as much about our employee attitudes.

Our entire management team is on board. Our HR Director is leading the effort.

EXAMPLE

What is a broader area of opportunity around this?

Reducing our company spending on health care

Want to keep the focus on wellness and our values, not just cost management.

What is a broader area of opportunity around this?

Improving employee engagement and productivity

Ask yourself
What's one reason this matters?

Reduce company-paid health care costs

START HERE
Current area of opportunity:

Improving the health of all employees through new wellness initiatives, programs, and/or other activities

This is it!

Ask yourself
What's another reason this matters?

Improve employee engagement and productivity

Ask yourself
What's one barrier that gets in the way?

Some of our leaders don't practice what we preach on employee wellness

Ask yourself
What's another barrier that gets in the way?

Many of our workers don't participate in health and wellness programs

What is a narrower area of opportunity focused on this?

Getting our entire management team to act as role models for healthy employee behavior

What is a narrower area of opportunity focused on this?

Increasing the participation rate in our existing programs

Too limited. We're not certain our existing programs meet everyone's needs.

EXAMPLE

Design Brief

Project Description	Improve the health of MRU employees to manage health care costs, increase productivity, and live the MRU values
Scope	Initial focus on US sites with 500+ employees Focus on existing employees (e.g., recruiting practices are out of scope)
Constraints	Comply with union/labor agreements Enable participation for employees from all shifts Maximum incremental budget of $250K
Target Users	MRU employees and their families Particular focus on current non-participants
Exploration Questions	Why do employees participate/not participate in current programs? What barriers to participation need to be addressed? What are some best practices? What are the biggest drivers of cost/health outcomes?
Expected Outcomes	Improved engagement and productivity Better health outcomes for employees Reduced health care premiums
Success Metrics	ROI of at least 2:1 At least 70% of employees participating in at least one element of our programs Health care premium increases due to plan spending not to exceed 2% year-on-year

EXAMPLE

People Plan

Makes me realize that I might need a different approach to get some management on board and to collaborate with our reps. A purely logical argument might not be enough to overcome some of their current perspective.

Stakeholder/User #1	Stakeholder/User #2	Stakeholder/User #3
Name Factory employees	Name Company management	Name Insurance reps
What is their current point of view? How will their behavior or actions need to be different in order to address my challenge? It's all over the map – we need to do some research here. Once we've addressed our challenge, every employee will take the actions needed to improve his/her health or wellness, whether through MRU's programs or not.	What is their current point of view? How will their behavior or actions need to be different in order to address my challenge? We've made it pretty easy for employees to get healthier. It's frustrating that so many employees don't take advantage of what we offer, especially since we invest so much. Some of our managers could be better role models for healthy living, and others may be inadvertently creating obstacles for their employees.	What is their current point of view? How will their behavior or actions need to be different in order to address my challenge? Our rates are already pretty low, but MRU continues to have at least a few employees with big claims each year. They've fully maxed out the wellness benefits of existing programs.
What am I curious about related to this stakeholder? Why don't people participate? Are there specific worries or barriers that we could address? What things are most helpful to our employees when making changes to their habits?	What am I curious about related to this stakeholder? Which of our programs do they personally participate in? How do they encourage their direct reports to live healthier lives? What's the biggest transformation they've seen in an employee?	What am I curious about related to this stakeholder? How will our reps be impacted if our insurance rates go up or down? What data about our company health can they provide? How does this stack up with their other clients? How much freedom do they have to help us develop new programs?
How can I develop empathy for this stakeholder? Remember when I got started with my workout routine and worked with a nutritionist. I stopped going after a few times; it was tough.	How can I develop empathy for this stakeholder? Think about when I tried to do something positive for my family and they didn't appreciate it or follow through. It made me a little cynical and less likely to stick to my program.	How can I develop empathy for this stakeholder? Consider how I feel about the customers I have who are always asking for more. I want to help, but it gets annoying after a while. Enough is enough!

EXAMPLE

Research Plan

Who or what will we study?	Where will we find the people or information?	What questions/issues will we explore?	Number of observations, interviews, or inputs	When will the research happen?	Who on the team is responsible?
Employees participating in wellness programs	Sampling of employees until we get enough in both areas	What's their definition of health? What programs do they participate in? What benefits do they see? What's still difficult or frustrating?	8	Next three weeks	Each team member conducts four interviews
Employees not participating in wellness programs	↓	What's their definition of health? What are the barriers to participating in programs? What has helped them form positive habits in the past? What do they wish was better about their health and wellness circumstances?	8	↓	↓
Market research about health and wellness	Online research; talk to our industry groups; talk to insurance reps	What are some best practices? What's new in corporate wellness programs? How are health care policies changing the landscape? What are key health trends?	N/A	Next two weeks	HR intern

EXAMPLE

Direct Observation

Observing utilization of onsite employee gym

Things to note (general)

- How many people come in each hour throughout the day?
- Which equipment is most utilized?
- Which equipment is least utilized?

Things to note (per individual observed)

- How long are they there?
- What activities do they do?
- What's their attitude or demeanor?
- Do they bring work or entertainment with them?
- How do they interact with others?
- Where is their progress stalled?

Interview Guide

Research Focus

Attitudes, beliefs, and behaviors regarding health and wellness

Information We're Seeking

Things we'd like to discuss with all participants include:

- What the words "health" and "wellness" mean to them
- What behaviors they associate with "health" and "wellness"
- What facilitates or inhibits healthy behaviors in their lives

Interview Questions

Explore the topics above using the following questions. In addition to these questions, use prompts such as "Tell me more," "What happened then?" and "What else?" to invite the participant to share more about his or her response. Silence (for about three seconds, just until it gets unbearably awkward) can also be a great way to learn more.

- Take a minute or two to tell me about yourself.
- What comes to mind when I say the word "wellness"?
- What comes to mind when I say the word "health"?

- When's the last time you did something that had an impact (positive or negative) on your health or wellness?

    - What did you do?
    - Tell me about it.
    - What prompted you to do that?
    - What impact did you notice?

- On a scale of 1 to 10, where 10 is the epitome of health, how would you characterize your current wellness?

    - What makes you rate it that way?
    - How does being a (insert rating) impact you?
    - How do you think a friend or family member might answer that question for you?
    - How would your doctor answer that question?
    - When is the last time you might have rated it higher or lower? What made it different then?

- Tell me a bit about your last visit to a doctor's office.

    - When was it?
    - What prompted your visit?
    - What happened?

- I'd like to learn a little bit about how health and wellness might fit into your life. Let's talk about a typical day for you. What's one day in the past week that you'd say was fairly typical?

    - Take a few minutes to walk me through that day, from when you woke up until when you called it a night.
    - How did you feel when you woke up in the morning? When you went to bed at the end of the day?
    - What was the best part of the day?
    - What was the worst or most frustrating part of the day?

- If you had a magic wand or could snap your fingers and change one thing you do that would positively impact your health and wellness, what would you do?

    - What would that do for you?
    - Have you tried doing that in the past? What happened?
    - What gets in the way when you try doing that (or when you imagine trying to do that)?

- Is there anything else you want to tell me about anything we've talked about today?

EXAMPLE

Posters

The full collection of posters include:

- 12 employee profiles
- 3 pages of direct observation data
- Current MRU program overview
- Current MRU program results
- Expert summary of dimensions of wellness
- 2 pages of best practice research regarding developing healthy habits
- Chart of average annual health insurance premiums
- Research summary of corporate wellness program best practices
- Quantitative research summary of most utilized aspects of corporate wellness programs
- Research study of U.S. employee attitudes about wellness programs

Jennifer

Health and Wellness Profile

Age: 42

Hometown: Columbus, OH

Family Status: married, with sons ages 7 and 11

Occupation: marketing specialist

Favorite Magazine: Conde Nast Traveler

Typical Attire: Ann Taylor, Banana Republic

Health and Wellness Status: "I'm tired all the time, but I think that's just being a mom. That, and the constant runny nose."

Wellness Goal: "It sounds strange, I know, but I'd love the peace and quiet of an hour at the gym a few times a week. OK, maybe not quiet."

"All day long, it's run, run, run. My husband and I get up at 5 to have coffee together. It's the only time we even really see each other. From the moment I wake Billy up at 7, it's nonstop."

"When the boys were little, we'd have playdates that were mostly us moms having coffee while our kids ran around. Being a soccer mom is a lot more work. It's worth it, but there's never a moment to get away. And when I do, I just feel guilty. There's always some mom thing that I could be doing. I fantasize about taking a cruise one day, just grown-ups."

"Having a clinic right near work is super convenient, especially when one or the other of the boys is sick. My doctor is way on the other side of town. Good thing I just have to get over there once or twice a year."

"Whatever I do, I want to know that it's worth it and the right thing for my family."

Wellness Program Offerings
Kaiser/HRET Surve

Among Firms Offering Health Benefits, Percen
Wellness Program to Their Employees, by Firm

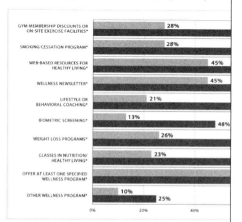

Source: Kaiser/HRET Survey of Employer-Sponsored Health Benefits, 19

Note: Biometric screening is a health examination that measures an em
blood pressure, stress, and nutrition. 2% of firms indicating "other" said
program (EAP) and 5% said that they offered flu shots.

Jared
Health and Wellness Profile

Age: 32

Hometown: Dallas, TX

Family Status: engaged

Occupation: business development analyst

Favorite Magazine: GQ, ESPN the Magazine

Typical Attire: a suit for work, Levi's mixed with men's fashion brands (Givenchy, Tom Ford) for leisure

Health and Wellness Status: "Haven't been to the doctor since college, but I feel fine. Maybe could stand to lose a few pounds. And I know I should quit smoking."

Wellness Goal: "Looking good on the beach for our honeymoon. And it would be nice to chill. Things have been crazy lately."

"I guess you'd say basketball is my thing. I played a little ball in college, and then had a regular pick-up game with some guys at the gym. But then I started missing games and I felt like a loser, so I stopped going."

"Some guys at the office and I have a pool going. For every day we don't make it to the gym, you put $1 in the pot. The last day of the month, it pays for our beer after work. It's probably a little sad that we always seem to have enough for a few rounds."

"Right now, aside from the wedding, I'm just thinking about work all the time. This is the time to get ahead, build a nest egg, buy a house. There will be time later to think about everything else. I just shouldn't have to worry about it now."

Persona Map

Solo

Prefers to keep health informaiton private and wants to pursue health and wellness on his or her own terms

Other axes considered included:

- desk-bound and mobile
- healthy and unhealthy
- enjoys exercise and doesn't enjoy exercise

- visited doctor within past year and didn't visit doctor in past year
- overweight and not overweight

MEET "I am what I am" Isabel
36-year-old single woman, moderately overweight since high school, practical minded, fiercely independent, and doesn't want anyone telling her what to do

Constrained by Logistics

Constrained by Desire

Wants to practice healthier habits but limited by time, funds, or other priorities

Content with current state of health and lacks motivation to adopt different habits

MEET "Tired Trudy"

28-year-old mother of twins who hasn't had time to herself in weeks, only sees her friends at work and when supervising playdates for their kids, spends time on message boards seeking parenting advice, wishes she had the energy to work out and regain her pre-pregnancy fitness levels, scared about her physical for life insurance

Each of these personas could inspire thinking about different needs and alternative types of solutions.

Seeks the support of others to manage health and wellness concerns

Social

360 Empathy

AREA OF OPPORTUNITY

OURS: Improving the health of all employees through new wellness initiatives, programs, and/or other activities

TRUDY'S: Getting back the body I had three years ago

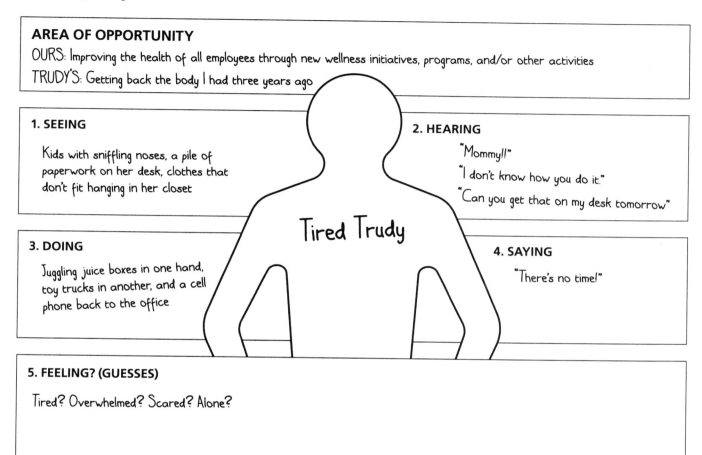

1. SEEING

Kids with sniffling noses, a pile of paperwork on her desk, clothes that don't fit hanging in her closet

2. HEARING

"Mommy!!"

"I don't know how you do it."

"Can you get that on my desk tomorrow"

3. DOING

Juggling juice boxes in one hand, toy trucks in another, and a cell phone back to the office

4. SAYING

"There's no time!"

Tired Trudy

5. FEELING? (GUESSES)

Tired? Overwhelmed? Scared? Alone?

6. LATENT NEED? (GUESSES)

Ease – To have her life simpler, more streamlined

Support – To make healthy choices as small changes

Movement – To engage in her own physical well-being

EXAMPLE

Job to Be Done

	Stakeholder's Desired Outcome	Metric of Success	Outcomes to Avoid
Functional Job	Lose weight Ability to keep up with the kids	Fit into clothes one size smaller Able to play a full game of tag with kids	Discomfort or continued alterations; looking bad Having to stop a game midway through; having to stop to catch my breath during play
Emotional Job	Feeling good about myself and how I look Finding ways to focus on me without feeling guilty	Liking what I see when I look in the mirror Looking forward to going to the beach Amount of fun time with the family doesn't decrease	Avoiding mirrors so I don't have to look at myself Family time suffering/husband and kids complaining

Value Chain

**Initial Inputs
to Value**

**Value Delivered
to Users**

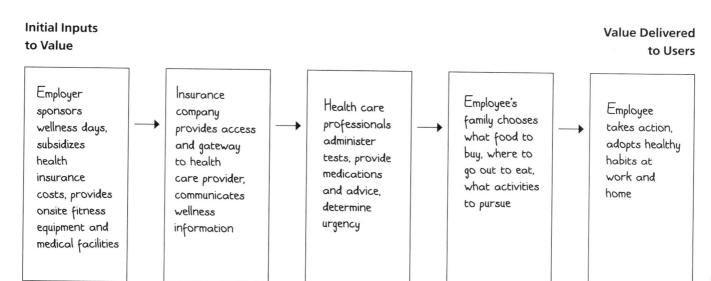

Mind Mapping

A group of five team members spent 30 minutes in the poster gallery and followed the mind-mapping process, clustering the data they gathered and using the clusters to help identify themes.

In the example shown here, there are a number of observations about people's relationships with their doctors. Upon reviewing the individual observations, the team noted that people's views about doctors weren't always positive and, in fact, were often a barrier to participating in MRU's wellness programs.

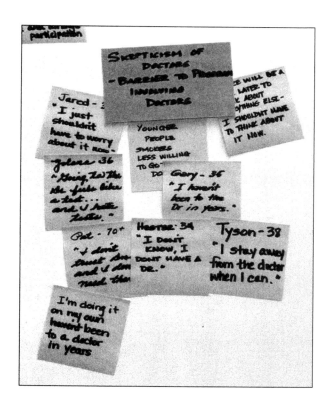

Design Criteria

If anything were possible, our new design would:

- Make people WANT to participate
- Provide easy access
- Facilitate social support
- Provide positive reinforcement
- Show visible early wins
- Attract employees most at risk for lifestyle-related health issues

Brainstorming

A group of three team members brainstormed using the blue-card technique and trigger questions.

Trigger Questions

- What could MRU do to improve the health and wellness of its employees?
- What efforts could MRU take to support the health and wellness of the 45% of its workforce, like Tired Trudy, that isn't participating in the wellness program?
- If Google were solving this problem for MRU, what would Google do to improve the health and wellness of MRU employees?
- Pick an institution that relies on a healthy workforce (e.g., military, sports teams). How could MRU draw inspiration from that institution?

T5 Online Health Assessments

Maximize online access to records + resources for mobil use

DIGITAL MEDICAL RECORDS

T5 ONLINE CHAT ROOMS

to exercise

T1 I have exercise classes on site

Company c w/ free f health

HEALTH INSURANCE DISCOUNT FOR ACTIVE PARTICIPATION IN PROGRAMS

T2 Discount on Health Insurance for participants

Low Cost Insurance

T1 HAVE PERSONAL TRAINERS ON SITE DURING WORK HOURS

Every 3rd

T2 MAKE NON-PARTICIPANTS PAY MORE FOR HEALTH INSURANCE

T1 Have nutrition classes on site during work hours

FOOD P HEA OPP

T1 Give people work time to engage in on-site programs

T4 ARMY HIRE NUTRITIONIST TO DESIGN MENUS IN CAFETERIA

Extensu Facilitu

T4 ARMY GIVE AWARDS TO THE MOST IMPROVED / INSPIRE OTHERS

T4 Army Schedule the time for wellness activities

Facili activit relat Fu

REWARD SYSTEM FOR BMI

Everyone must participate (at their level of ability)

TESTED + ENFORCED STANDARDS / not FITNESS - JOB DESCRIPTION

allow EEs to spend 20% of working time exercising

Team Based

ELIMINATE SMOKING

Mandatory PT

Targeted Education on Benefits

Program is opt-out not opt-in

T2 Have a "buddy" program so coworkers help motivate

Gym/ Nutritionist available to immediately / ufamily

Strong sense of community

PROVIDE /HR OF TIME PER DAY DURING WK HRS FOR EXERCISE

BRING A FRIEND FOR FREE

Forced Connections

AREA OF OPPORTUNITY   Creating an engaging way for MRU employees to improve their health + wellness.

Idea 1

Tap into peer pressure for healthy living by publicly listing health "winners" and "losers"

Idea 3

Have the company nutritionist "audit" people's lunches

Issue pedometers to employees and require a minimum number of steps per day

Idea 2

Forced Connection Concept 1

Sponsor an annual team fitness challenge, with participation open to all and required for all members of the management team. Each manager is responsible for recruiting a team of 6 people to walk the equivalent distance of a cross-country trek. Participants are issued pedometers and log their miles daily, and a leaderboard in the lobby updates results weekly. The winning team gets a company-provided lunch every Friday for a year.

Forced Connection Concept 2

Award departments a team bonus if all their employees participate in the MRU wellness program and complete a confidential medical screening. Individuals in a department can earn their team "points" good for an additional bonus (or to offset a member's refusal to participate) by volunteering in other healthy activities, like increasing their average daily step count or having the nutritionist monitor their food log or "screen" their lunches to make healthy substitutions.

Forced Connection Concept 3

Create a company standard for walking. Give every employee a pedometer and have HR coordinate initiatives to increase movement at work (e.g., walking meetings, no phone/email days) and healthy eating at work (e.g., lunchbox audits, unhealthy food swaps, healthy vending machines). Publish a weekly top-to-bottom ranking of the management team and the top 10 employee walkers.

Chili Table

CATEGORIES

Food	Exercise	Lifestyle	Employment	Incentive

IDEAS

Food	Exercise	Lifestyle	Employment	Incentive
Put healthy food in vending machines Provide healthy lunches — Have MRU nutritionist develop menus Host cooking classes as team-building sessions Make "meatless Mondays" in the cafeteria	Implement five-minute stretch breaks every hour Get all employees to walk more on the job Eliminate conference rooms and host walking meetings Require that every employee enter the fitness center at least once a week	Start a diabetes support group Sponsor intramural sports teams Subsidize errand services for employees (dry cleaning, house cleaning, grocery shopping, etc.)	Explain health expectations as part of hiring process Make participation in wellness program a requirement for employment	Give people bonuses for healthy behaviors at work Have a weight loss contest Hold a drawing for everyone who uses the fitness center

Concept: Conduct an MRU-friendly "Biggest Losers" program, where the "hosts" are our corporate nutritionists and they coach people on and off the job. Nutritionists coordinate with errand company on foods to purchase for people.

EXAMPLE

EXAMPLE

Napkin Pitch

CONCEPT NAME: America's Healthiest Company Contest

The Big Idea

An employee weight loss contest, based on the TV show "The Biggest Loser"

Use nutritionists as coaches; senior management as judges

Make it social — create opportunity for whole company to be involved/share tips/encourage

Add incentives to get everyone involved — departments win along with their contestants

Build healthy activities and eating into the work day — open to everyone as well as contestants

Needs/Benefits

Create fun and motivation through the fanfare and competition of the contest for unmotivated "I am who I am" Isabel types

Build it into the work day for time-pressed "Tired Trudy" types

Social dimension gets everyone involved

Weekly weight loss tallies will provide visible wins

Rewards success versus punishing failure

Execution

Take advantage of electronic suggestion box to solicit entry forms

Company newsletter, announcements in gym, postings in cafeteria can all be used to promote the contest

Offer ongoing counseling to keep weight off

Can leverage existing wellness offerings to assist contestants

Partner with local Weight Watchers organization to provide structure and support

Partner with local organic grocery to feature healthy eating opportunities at work — and to carry home

Business Rationale

Employee weight loss will improve incidence of diabetes, heart disease, and other weight-sensitive maladies, lowering medical costs

Healthy-weight employees may be more productive and energetic

Create a company-wide esprit de corps

Key Assumptions

CONCEPT NAME: America's Healthiest Company Contest		TE	2D/ 3D	4D
VALUE TEST • Customers want it • Customers will pay for it • Partners want it	At-risk employees will try out the program + stick with it		X	
	Social element will be viewed positively, as a game		X	
	Lower-risk employees will participate; no stigma		X	
EXECUTION TEST • We can produce the experience technically • We can acquire customers • We can operate the business as it grows	Intra-net contest won't violate HIPAA	X		
	MRU can hire and manage external counselors		X	
	MRU can create a safe on-ramp for employees to try it			X
SCALE TEST • Addressable market is big enough • We can acquire customers affordably • Revenues exceed costs at scale	We can handle demand if 2/3 of employees participate	X		
	This will continue to be funded			X
DEFENSIBILITY TEST • We can protect advantage • Advantage increases as we grow the business	N/A			

THOUGHT EXPERIMENT

- Learn through analysis of existing data
- Typical time frame: one or two days
- No exposure to third parties required

2D & 3D SIMULATION EXPERIMENT

- Learn through dialog with market participants using storyboards or prototypes
- Typical time frame: one or two weeks
- May require us to expose our intentions to selected market participants

LIVE (4D) IN-MARKET EXPERIMENT

- Test via a live experience of the offering (e.g., a 30-day live trial)
- Typical time frame: 30 to 90 days
- Requires us to expose our offering to many market participants

EXAMPLE

Storytelling

Meet ... **Tired Trudy.**	*hero / user*
She is a ... **mother of young twins**	*role*
with a penchant for ... **daydreaming about exotic beach vacations**	*personal attribute*
who wants to ... **survive until her boys are in elementary school and fit into her pre-pregnancy clothes one day.**	*goal*
One day she is at ... **work during lunch**	*setting*
and she tries to ... **make a meal plan for her family so she can stop at the grocery store on her way home.**	*move toward goal*
Instead of ... **coming up with some healthy meals for her family,**	*intended outcome*
she discovers ... **that she can't find any recipes that both her boys and her husband will enjoy.**	*obstacle*
Now she must ... **go to the store and wing it, which she knows will probably lead to more chicken tenders for the kids and chinese takeout for her and husband.**	*complication*
Just when she feels ... **overwhelmed and like she'll never have energy again,**	*authentic emotion*
she is surprised to discover ... **that MRU provides meal planning for participants in the Healthiest Company contest.**	*unexpected ally – your solution*
Suddenly ... **she wonders whether she might find the time to get to the gym if someone else is there to help with the other stuff.**	*path to goal*
Today she is able to ... **make smarter choices about her family's meals and spend her lunch hours working out instead of scouring parenting websites,**	*simple path to goal*
and she can realize ... **she's on her way to feeling better about her health and more in control of her life.**	*higher-level goal or need*

Learning Launch Design

Key Assumptions to Test	Learning Launch # __1__
People won't be embarrassed and will want to sign up The people who most need to lose weight will sign up Peer pressure will be a positive force, rather than an anxiety-producing one	**Who** Employees at two different plant locations in the US **Where** Small factory or office locations where we have confidence in HR staff to run the contest and monitor progress and effects **How** Design two separate contests: one has the social dimension and emphasizes peer involvement and support; the other makes the contest a more personal, private event Collect metrics on those who sign up: weight loss goal, health status Interview contestants throughout contest (possibly using an online diary) about why they signed up, what their concerns are, and what they believe contributes most to their success Assess likely health-related outcomes change at end, in addition to weight loss (e.g. lower blood pressure, cholesterol) **Cost** Opportunity costs of staff time to set up and monitor: approximately 100 hours per location Out-of-pocket expenditures for additional support not currently offered at those locations — gym classes, nutritional counseling, upgrade in cafeteria healthy offerings: $5000 per location Cost of rewards given to winning employee and department (in social group): $1000 **Time** Run experiment for three months, monitor continuing effects for six additional months

EXAMPLE

What to Watch For

Untested Assumptions	Success Metric	Disconfirming Data
People will not be too embarrassed by all the attention and will want to participate	A lot of employees signing up	Few sign-ups
The employees who need to lose weight the most for health-related reasons will sign up	Average number of desired pounds to lose is significant relative to body weight	The people who sign up are generally in good shape already and only need to lose 10 or so pounds
Involving peers will be a good thing, providing support in a positive way	Contestants will feel supported in a positive way	Contestants feel worried about how others will react if they fail; peer pressure makes them anxious

Acknowledgments

We would like to acknowledge the ongoing support of the Batten Institute for Innovation and Entrepreneurship at the University of Virginia Darden School of Business. Without their funding and encouragement, this work would not have been possible.

A project of this nature demands co-creation with users and iteration of several prototypes. We would like to thank our friends at Mars, Incorporated for supporting our efforts and putting early prototypes of this field book into managers' hands. It's appropriate that we were able to practice design thinking in the development of our design thinking work.